PRAISE FOR

THE SHOCKING TRUTH
Behind What Men
REALLY Think About Women

"Having led teams at the highest levels, I know the value of understanding diverse perspectives. Sandy Camillo provides a rare and honest look into what men really think about women, making this book an invaluable resource for leaders and decision-makers."

—Robert Romasco, Past President of AARP

"In my personal experience, *THE SHOCKING TRUTH Behind What Men REALLY Think About Women* sheds light on conversations many shy away from. The book is a bold, necessary exploration of the way men truly perceive women, offering revelations that can help reshape our societal narratives."

—Gloria L. Blackwell, CEO of AAUW (American Association of University Women), endorsing in a personal capacity

"A revealing and thought-provoking exploration of men's perspectives on women, this book challenges societal norms and offers valuable insights—essential for anyone committed to advancing gender equality and understanding through open dialogue."

—Devin Thorpe, CEO, The Super Crowd, Inc., a public benefit corporation

"Sandy Camillo's insights into male-female dynamics are astute and sophisticated, making *THE SHOCKING TRUTH* an invaluable resource for HR professionals, managers, and therapists. Her understanding of gender psychology beautifully explores the unique ways men and women think, feel, and act. This book is both educational and essential for work and home. I eagerly await its release to share with my patients and colleagues!"

—Christopher Bayer, PhD, The Wall Street Psychologist

"Breaking barriers in a male-dominated industry like regulation crowdfunding has given me unique insights into how men value women. This book offers a candid, eye-opening perspective, providing a path to deeper connection, respect, and equality. This book is an invaluable resource and essential reading for today's world."

—Ruth E. Hedges, CEO of Rise UP Crowdfunding, coined by Fortune as the Queen of Crowdfunding

"In this refreshing, conversation-starting book, Camillo effectively incorporates diverse perspectives on gender socialization . . . A provocative book that asks important questions."

—*Kirkus Reviews*

THE SHOCKING TRUTH Behind What Men REALLY Think About Women
by Sandy Camillo

© Copyright 2025 Sandy Camillo

979-8-88824-702-0

All rights reserved. No part of this publication may be reproduced, stored in a retrieval system, or transmitted in any form or by any means—electronic, mechanical, photocopy, recording, or any other—except for brief quotations in printed reviews, without the prior written permission of the author.

Designed by Suzanne Bradshaw.

Published by

köehlerbooks™

3705 Shore Drive
Virginia Beach, VA 23455
800-435-4811
www.koehlerbooks.com

The
SHOCKING TRUTH

Behind What **MEN** *REALLY* Think About **WOMEN**

SANDY CAMILLO

VIRGINIA BEACH
CAPE CHARLES

To my father, whose constant presence and unwavering support nurtured in me the values of strength, equality, and respect. You believed deeply in the potential of each of your children, aspiring for us all to thrive, regardless of whether we were daughters or sons. Your admiration for women and steadfast encouragement have been the guiding lights in my life. Though you are no longer with us, your legacy endures and is a beacon of integrity and respect for all men to emulate.

Table of Contents

PREFACE 1

INTRODUCTION 3

CHAPTER 1 9
MOM KNOWS BEST, OR IS IT SOME OTHER
WOMAN IN MY LIFE?

CHAPTER 2 26
DO MEN THINK WOMEN ARE EQUAL? DEPENDS
ON WHO'S PAYING FOR DINNER.

CHAPTER 3 44
ROSES ARE RED, VIOLETS ARE BLUE, BUT WHAT
THE HECK IS ROMANCE? I WISH THAT I KNEW.

CHAPTER 4 59
THE FEMALE ATTRIBUTES THAT
DRIVE MEN WILD

CHAPTER 5 75
SMARTY PANTS OR HOT PANTS:
WHAT TURNS A MAN ON?

CHAPTER 6 91
SHE'S GOT THE MONEY, HONEY;
BUT WHO WEARS THE PANTS?

CHAPTER 7 102
WHAT TURNS WOMEN ON?
A DREAMY SMILE OR A BMW?

CHAPTER 8 119
HOT BABE TO UGLY HAG. HOW LOOKS AFFECT
THE FICKLE NATURE OF ATTRACTION

CHAPTER 9 137
THE FRIEND ZONE:
WHERE A MAN'S DREAMS GO TO DIE

CHAPTER 10 150
ARE YOU NUTS:
A FEMALE DOCTOR?

CHAPTER 11 169
THE GREAT DEBATE:
BEYOND APRONS AND LULLABIES

CHAPTER 12 183
FROM CAVEMEN
TO WOKENESS

AFTERWORD 197
Acknowledgments 205
Bibliography 206

PREFACE

LET'S BE HONEST. When it comes to physical appearance, men are often drawn to a woman with a perfect figure instead of her intelligence or personality. There are few men either brave or stupid enough to publicly admit holding such prurient criteria in their estimation of a woman's value. But don't be fooled by the socially correct answers you hear from men about how they perceive women. Behind their mask of civility lies a world of primal impulses and unspoken biases. What if we could peek behind this wall of silence and discover the truth about what men truly think about women?

Women often struggle for visibility in a world rife with gender bias, but they have started to discover ways for their voices to be heard so they can battle gender discrimination. Now it's time to give men the same chance to speak out.

For too long, men have been held to an idealized prototype of being physically strong, emotionally shallow, and driven to succeed at all costs. But the reality is often different. Many men find it difficult to express their true feelings about the women in their lives, and this book aims to change that. It explores the male psyche, exposing whether men's impressions of women are governed solely by their primal impulses, or whether there is another dynamic at play influencing their thoughts about women.

Can a woman relate to the men in her life if she is only seeing the artificial male version molded by society? Would a male-female relationship change if a woman discovered a man's true thoughts about her? The few books written on what men think about women are either thirty years old and outdated or written from the author's personal perspective without any objective reference. In contrast, *THE SHOCKING TRUTH Behind What Men REALLY Think About Women* is based on two independent, anonymous surveys, one of men and another of women, as well as historical narratives on this topic. The chapters also include conversations between three fictional male friends that occur during their monthly meetup at a neighborhood bar. Each man presents a unique perspective in his responses to the questions posed in the survey. The findings gathered from these diverse sources will surprise both men and women. Women will find out the truth about what men honestly think of them, and men might find some comfort when they discover that they are not alone in their views about women.

So, buckle up and get ready to discover what lies behind this wall of silence. However, this book is not for the faint of heart but for those willing to explore the raw and unfiltered truth about men's deepest desires and prejudices about women.

INTRODUCTION

I AM A voracious reader with the attention span of a fruit fly. Although I am fascinated with surveys, I rarely am able to delve through massive volumes of statistical results without starting to feel jumpy, unless the results are intermingled with personal anecdotes. I believe that there are many of you out there who, like me, either lack patience or focus to read something that is too academic, regardless of the importance of the content.

Although I'd like to think that discovering what men really think about women is a stimulating concept for a book, simply reporting survey results would probably lull most people to sleep. With that thought in mind, I tried to spice up the conveyance of this information in my book, *THE SHOCKING TRUTH Behind What Men REALLY Think About Women* by blending fact and fiction in each chapter. The material in each chapter focuses on questions taken from an anonymous survey conducted by Survey Monkey, an independent third party responsible for survey distribution and data collection. The subject matter of each chapter is divided into three sections that first presents a fictional narrative highlighting the personal accounts of three men, followed by a historical perspective, and finally, the results of the surveys.

The survey participants are of different ages, races, religions, careers, ethnicities, educational and economic backgrounds. To provide a universal perspective, participants queried were from the United States, as well as other countries. Because the survey is anonymous the answers revealing men's feelings and perceptions about women are assumed to be truthful, as the male participants don't have to fear retribution from angry women. A secondary survey with women respondents is also included using the same questions contained in the men's survey. Women guessed the men's responses. The comparison of the two surveys shows whether women have any idea of what men truthfully think about them.

Before the results of the surveys are revealed, we'll eavesdrop on conversations between three fictional characters, Jim, Buddy, and Noah, as they each talk about their relationship with women. Then we'll travel through time from the biblical age to the present day by sharing stories that illustrate men's attitudes toward women. For example, remember the story of Adam and Eve in that garden? We can never know what they really thought about each other, and yet the story is that Adam joined Eve in eating the forbidden fruit. Clearly, there was something about Eve that intrigued Adam enough to risk the wrath of God. Perhaps my book will reveal what that something was, and whether Adam's male descendants, like our fictional characters Jim, Buddy, and Noah, followed in the first human male's footsteps in their interactions with women, or whether early men forged their own path in dealing with the women in their lives. Finally, after our travels through history are complete, you'll get the actual answers of the survey respondents.

You might be thinking that unless I've been reincarnated several times, there's no way that I could know the thoughts of men from past generations. Although it's true that I can't go back in time to administer a survey to men, I have looked into documented records dating back from biblical times to the present day that cite the prevalent behavior of men in their interactions with women. This behavior gives us an indication of the underlying attitude of these men toward women. However, it's somewhat difficult to judge whether these actions truly reflect the beliefs of the men, or if they were simply conforming to the expectations of society at the time. We've all heard the saying that actions speak louder than words, but actions don't always tell the entire story. There is some debate as to whether men are biologically wired to act as the dominant partner in a relationship. If so, are their attitudes toward women preordained? I'm sure many men would jump for joy if the winner in such a debate was on the side of biological determination.

For my female readers, I have some advice about several possible consequences of your reading this book. First, take a deep breath and imagine yourself in a happy place. Some of the men's responses might make you wonder if the men in your lives are actually strangers. This may provide you with many hours of excitement as you explore who these men truly are. You also might feel guilty that you never took the time to encourage your men to express their true selves to you. On the other hand, you might decide to tell some of your men that they should live alone in a cave with bats as their only companions.

Men reading my book might identify with some of the startling revelations in the survey and sigh with relief that they won't ignite into a ball of fire by admitting to similar feelings about women. Maybe they will feel liberated and even let their tears flow without feeling emasculated while watching a sad movie together with one of the women in their lives. They might finally even be able to reject society's expectation that a *real* man must single-handedly carry the weight of the world on his shoulders.

—

LET'S START OUR story by first meeting our fictional characters, Jim, Buddy, and Noah who are sitting together at a bar for one of their monthly get-togethers. All three of these imagined men are in their forties. They grew up together in a nondescript suburb in the Northeast and have remained best friends.

Although their childhood backgrounds are similar, their adult lives have taken divergent paths, and correspondently their viewpoints on various topics differ considerably.

Jim is a hedge-fund guy who is riding high on the income he's earned from a booming stock market. His appearance epitomizes the world of high finance in America that was personified by Gordon Gekko in the film *Wall Street*. He wears Brioni suits and Gucci loafers, and just recently bought himself a Hermès Carré watch. Even his casual wear reeks of luxury. He maintains his fit physique by working out at an exclusive health club five times a week and has a standing appointment every two weeks with his barber to keep his dark mane impeccably manicured. If he has a really important meeting coming up, he'll even schedule a manicure. He's always been a go-getter, determined to make money and climb the corporate ladder. He is married and has one child. Although he's friendly, his ambitions sometimes prevent him from developing meaningful relationships outside of his immediate family.

Buddy is a freight truck driver and lifelong member of the Teamsters Union. He has an extensive collection of tee shirts and sweatshirts to wear with his jeans, which he pairs with his well-worn Timberland boots. His long hair hasn't changed much from the style he had in high school. The only concession that he makes for his job is to pull his graying frock back into a ponytail. Buddy has never seen the inside of a gym, and yet he is trim from all the heavy lifting that he does on the job. His manner and appearance imply that he's a man's man who's not afraid to get grimy. Despite his rough exterior, Buddy is a kind and loyal friend. Buddy has never been married and has no desire to change that status. He's not afraid to speak his mind and offer practical, if not socially conscious, perspectives to his buddies.

The self-professed intellectual in the group is Noah, who is a philosophy professor at an Ivy League college. He's an excellent listener and always eager to learn and explore new ideas. He prides himself on being relatable to his students but realizes that his pledges must also respect him and embrace his authority. His youthful looks belie his chronological age, and many times he has been mistaken for a student. Although he doesn't adopt the Hollywood version of a typical Ivy League professor's attire of cardigan sweater, bow tie, suit jacket, and glasses, he still tries to appear professorial by favoring button-down collar shirts, penny loafers, and occasionally a blazer. The first thing that people remark on when they meet Noah is that he is incredibly handsome. He could stand in as a double for Ryan Gosling, and yet his self-effacing manner belies that he isn't vain. His boyish charm is genuine, and his interactions with women are guided by his admiration of their gender. Although he's not married, he is in a long-term, exclusive relationship with his girlfriend.

Although Jim, Buddy, and Noah differ in their perception of gender roles in the world, there is one thing that they all agree on—the enjoyment that they get from being with each other. Their monthly get-togethers always end in raucous laughter as they tackle provocative world issues. Each month, the trio agree to focus on one subject to discuss. The only condition for their chats is that they are brutally honest in their responses.

ON THIS NIGHT, the men's laughter is subdued as the topic of their conversation fills them with a sense of apprehension. The cause of this trepidation is, perhaps, a fear that their conversation will veer in a direction that could jeopardize all they hold dear in life. Yet as the night goes on, they become increasingly talkative as the huge amounts of alcohol they've imbibed loosen their tongues. They are entering a zone where only dialogue conforming to society's socially accepted mores is permitted—what they really think about women.

Jim, Buddy, and Noah experience that rush of bravado that often accompanies their familiar sense of camaraderie. They finally decide to tackle the subject that they planned to discuss that night and that they had long been avoiding. Can they be honest about something that could result in ruined relationships, bruised egos, and accusations of misogyny? Noah made the first overture into the conversation.

"Do you know what drives me crazy about my girlfriend, Jane?"

And so our journey begins.

CHAPTER 1

MOM KNOWS BEST, OR IS IT SOME OTHER WOMAN IN MY LIFE?

Fear grips our hearts when we notice rapidly flashing lights in our rearview mirror accompanied by the dreaded sound of a yelping siren. Most of us ask ourselves, "Are the police after me?" We start wondering what we could have done wrong to have the police signal us to pull our car off the road. We start to regret that second drink that we had at the party. Chances are that you've heard of getting a DUI, although hopefully, you've never personally gotten one. Driving under the influence of alcohol can result in several negative consequences such as injury, arrest, and imprisonment. It's undeniable that alcohol can instigate a person to do incredibly stupid things, but there are also other more obscure influencing determinants that can have major positive and negative effects on a person's life.

A person can be coerced into doing something they might not do voluntarily. For example, if someone pushes you off a building ledge, it's obvious that you have been directly compelled by force to fall. However, chances are that you'd jump off a building ledge if someone threatened to shoot your child unless you did so. This hypothetical may seem overly dramatic when comparing a woman's influence on a man's life, but the point here is that men throughout the ages have experienced joy, misery, fame, ruination, mental collapse, and death because of a woman's influence.

Before we examine the real-life stories of men and women from yesterday and today, let's eavesdrop on our three fictional characters Jim, Buddy, and Noah as they sit together in a bar, discussing their thoughts about something contained in the first survey question, namely which woman they think most influenced their lives.

Our hedge-fund guy, Jim, is doing his best to explain to Buddy and Noah the circumstances that led him for many years to believe that a woman's place was in the home. Speaking to his two friends, he tells them, "I am the youngest child in a family of four children. One of my brothers is a renowned heart surgeon, and the other is a United States federal court judge. My mom worked for a brief time solely to support the family so my dad could complete law school. She stopped working once he got his first job at a Wall Street firm. My sister copied my mom's life story by getting married while she was still in high school and became the mother of two sons by the time she celebrated her 20th birthday. Both my mother and sister are seemingly content with their roles as stay-at-home moms, which led me to believe that all women dreamed of having similar lives. My assumption has resulted in grave discord between my wife and me, as I can't understand why she wishes to return to work now that our daughter is about to graduate from high school."

Struggling to find the words to express his thoughts to his friends without sounding mushy, Jim continues. "I've attained financial success in my life as judged by my seven-figure salary, so I don't understand my wife's motivation for a return to work, as we certainly don't need the money. This argument about my wife's possible return to work had been going on for months until one evening, after we had a particularly vicious fight, I retreated to my office and flipped the light switch on. Someone was sitting in the room waiting for me. That someone was Beth, my eighteen-year-old daughter. Evidently, she had been listening to my latest battle with my wife and had decided to share with me her perspective on a woman's role in society. Beth asked me if I would have married and had a child if it meant that I would be prohibited from attaining success in my chosen profession and, instead, was required to spend my life eternally cooking, cleaning, and taking care of a child. She further wanted to know if my love for her and her mother was diminished because I was fulfilled by the work I did outside the home. Beth reminded me that when my sister and I were babies, we both required nourishment, shelter, sleep, and love. Our different genders didn't affect our need for these necessities. She asked me if I thought that my quest for personal fulfillment was more important than my sister's, or my mother's. Then, to my great surprise, Beth told me that she planned on following a science curriculum in college so that she could follow her dream of becoming a scientist."

Jim hoped that he wasn't sharing too much with his friends but thought it was important that he continue. "I felt like a lightbulb had suddenly been turned on in my head and this light illuminated a new mindset regarding gender roles. I realized that although my mother and sister had found fulfillment in being stay-at-home moms, many women had goals in life that required the pursuit of a career track outside of the home. The motivations for these career women didn't center solely on monetary gain, although they enjoyed the income. Instead, something was driving them to discover new horizons. My mother and sister greatly influenced me in developing an appreciation of their chosen path in life, but it was Beth who influenced me to change perspective. She taught me to reject gender bias regarding a woman's role in society and to respect the concept of the individuality and equality of men and women."

Jim took a deep breath and turned to Buddy and said, "My wife, Claire, starts her new job on Tuesday. I'll let you know then how it feels to take over some of the household duties. Now why don't you tell us how a macho man like you was influenced by a woman in your life."

BUDDY TOLD JIM and Noah that he loved driving trucks and being a part of the Teamsters Union. He said, "I'm a road warrior who doesn't have to answer to anyone. I swear that I'll never be tied down to one woman. Women have told me that this doesn't make me a very desirable boyfriend. However, I believe that women exist to act as helpmates to men and to help them relax when they get too wound up. Unfortunately, my philosophy riles up many women."

As I listened in on this conversation, I thought that the term "chauvinist" aptly described Buddy. But before I could expand my thoughts, Buddy continued his explanation to Jim and Noah. "I know that women won full membership in the Teamsters Union in 1943 because of their efforts working in the factory production lines during World War II. They performed a great patriotic service to our country, enabling men to go off to war and fight. Despite this, I still consider the Teamsters a haven where men can be men. This was my mantra until one day my foreman suddenly died of a heart attack and word quickly spread that our new foreman would be a woman. After making several inquiries, I discovered that the rumor was correct. I heard that the men who worked alongside this woman raved about her productivity because she always took on the most difficult jobs and worked the longest hours. I was still concerned that my boys' club was about to be invaded and that the risqué jokes and behavior would be a thing of the past because my new boss would now be a woman."

Buddy recalled the day that the female forewoman was meeting with her subordinates. He was waiting to be called into her office. He was determined to be himself throughout the meeting. He admitted to Jim and Noah that it appeared that his chauvinistic reputation preceded him. Once seated in her office, the forewoman immediately asked Buddy to express his misgivings about having a female boss. Buddy told his friends, "I was startled at her candor, and I blurted out how I and my coworkers accepted each other's foibles and vulgarities because we all shared many of the same male characteristics, sometimes considered undesirable by women. I was concerned that I would now have to become someone other than my true self. The forewoman asked me if being my true self meant always letting it all hang loose, and if so, would I be comfortable if my female coworkers also hung loose and loudly engaged in daily discussions of certain feminine topics such as menopause and cesarian childbirths? I shook my head disdainfully and told my new boss that there's no place for things like that in the workplace. 'Right you are,' she said. For the first time in many years, my ingrained thoughts about women in the workforce were being challenged."

Buddy explained, "The forewoman influenced the way that I had always thought about workplace dynamics, and most importantly, she elicited from me my judgment on proper behavior in the workplace. After the situation was flipped around to reflect feminine considerations, I could finally see my behavior from a woman's perspective. Part of me has to admit that many times, women get treated unfairly when they're on the job. Okay, now I guess it's time to hear from Noah, our prim and proper professor."

—

NOAH BLANCHED AT hearing Buddy's description of him as "prim and proper" as Noah knew that his persona with his friends didn't reflect his true nature. Noah decided that it was time to tell Jim and Buddy about his relationship with his girlfriend, Jane, and admit how her influence saved him from developing an unsavory reputation and suffering the possible death of his career. "I met Jane," he said, speaking in a subdued voice, when I was teaching philosophy at Columbia. Jane was my student in an honor class for seniors. She engaged in subtle flirtations with me, and to be honest I got a real thrill out of her attention. Her flirtations were obvious to anyone watching us. One person watching was uncomfortable by what she saw and reported our behavior to my supervisor. But I managed to convince the supervisor that nothing inappropriate was happening between me and Jane."

"Perhaps early on," Noah hesitantly continued, "I had convinced myself that our infatuation with each other was just innocent, but before too long I became deeply involved with Jane, and after her graduation, we began a torrid love affair. I understand now that part of my original fascination for Jane centered on the forbidden erotic nature of our professor-student status. Although Jane and I are seriously committed to one another, she still has trust issues stemming from the inherent power imbalance that existed at the beginning of our relationship and my obvious willingness to ignore university prohibitions that restrict consensual professor-student relationships."

Noah went on. "Jane is now worried that in the future, there could be another young female student adoringly gazing into my eyes as she memorizes every pearl of wisdom that leaves my lips, and before I realize it, I will again be entangled with a student romantically. Jane is also mature enough now to realize that my moral compass might be a little screwed up and lead me to become a repeat offender. Therefore, Jane gave me an ultimatum: I could get therapy, or she would be out of my life. Since I love Jane and realize that my sometimes-uncontrollable attraction to pretty women could get me into trouble, I decided to see a therapist. Jane's influence saved me from potentially losing the love of my life and my profession."

After listening to these conversations, it's obvious that the lives of Jim, Buddy, and Noah have been greatly influenced by women who represent three different female roles— a daughter, boss, and love interest. In the next part of our story, we'll begin our exploration of how other men were influenced by women throughout history.

YESTERDAY

People are influenced by many factors, including emotions such as fear, hate, love, and lust. In addition, the desire for fame, prestige, and financial gain, societal expectations, moral imperatives, peer pressure, conformity, and spiritual beliefs all exert a powerful sway on the direction of a person's life. These factors often vary depending on the societal norms of each distinct historical era.

For example, men and women in Ancient Egypt and Rome wore loincloths as both underwear and outer clothing, having been influenced by the clothing standards of the time. In present times, one of the few ways to see a man wearing a loincloth is to attend a Sumo wrestling competition, where the participants are decked out in the traditional Mawashi (loincloth). Thus, societal influence has resulted in major changes in men's fashion over the decades. However, my research indicates surprisingly little change throughout history in men's responses to the question of which woman most influenced their lives.

Obviously, I wasn't personally present to hear the voices of men living in ancient times. However, written history captures the essence of their feelings. As we travel together through a few different eras to discover how women influenced men, it seems most fitting to begin our narrative with the story of Adam, the first man on earth. Although your trust in the veracity of this story may depend on your religious or spiritual beliefs, let's assume for the moment that the story actually occurred.

The story of Adam and Eve is told in the book of Genesis. Moses is credited as being the author of this book. Typically, the sentiment of an author is reflected in his or her writing. Therefore, we need to look at the life of Moses, the assumed author, for clues as to whether his attitude toward women was reflected in his story of Adam and Eve.

History tells us that when Moses headed back to Egypt with his wife and sons, he met up with the Lord who tried to kill him. At great danger to her own safety, Moses's wife, Zipporah, interceded to save him and yet, despite her loyalty, she was cast aside by Moses, and she and her children were sent away. Moses doesn't come out of this story smelling like roses, but the end result is that Moses was then unencumbered to lead the exodus of the Israelites out of Egypt and to become a biblical hero. His stirring story demonstrates a woman's powerful influence on not only a man's existence, but also on important world events. Unfortunately, in the end, Zipporah was rejected by Moses.

In the story of Adam and Eve, Moses reveals the great influence that Eve exerted over Adam. Conversely, unlike Moses's treatment of his wife, Adam's loyalty to Eve was unwavering. The story of Adam and Eve underscores Adam's subjugation of his will to Eve. This results in Adam's relinquishment of paradise in exchange for being with Eve. The outcome of Eve's influence on Adam, contrary to Moses's experience, shows the sometimes-disastrous consequences of a woman's influence. There is no hesitancy in Adam's disobedience of God's orders. Adam's words, "The woman you gave to be with me—she gave me some fruit from the tree, and I ate." This incontestably shows where his loyalties lie (Gen. 3:12). Evidently, Adam's words explaining why he ate the fruit from the forbidden tree in the garden of Eden makes it clear that he was influenced by his love for his wife beyond even the fear of God's retribution. Of course, one must wonder if Eve's influence would have been so commanding if there were other women around.

The stories of Adam and Moses show us the substantial influence that wives can have over their husbands. However, historical sources show us that wives weren't the only women responsible for influencing their men. Throughout history, stories abound about the influence of mothers on their sons and the sometimes-earth-shaking consequences of these interactions.

Looking back at some mother-son relationships throughout the centuries, it's easy to understand the reason why mothers had such great influence on their sons. Such mothers wielded enormous influence on their sons because the sons made it clear them that they would do anything for them. Mothers of some great leaders of the Middle Ages begged, threatened, and even engaged in nefarious acts to help their sons retain power or to maintain family harmony. Some mothers like the Anglo-Saxon Queen Elfrida even murdered her stepson so her biological son could succeed to the throne as king. Genghis Khan was known as one of the fiercest rulers of his time and yet he was a teddy bear when it came to his mother's influence on him. Because of his great love and respect for his mother, Hoelun acquiesced to her exhortations not to execute his brother for treason.

Skipping ahead several decades, most mothers' influence no longer centered on murder and mayhem, and yet many of the greatest leaders still attribute their success to their mothers. Interestingly, even big, hulking, solemn-looking men held surprisingly tender feelings for their mothers. Abraham Lincoln was one such man. He was assassinated on Good Friday, which led many people to associate him with a kind of sainthood. He, in turn, attributed his success to his "angel" mother in his words, "All that I am, or hope to be, I owe to my angel mother" (Deseret News). Although he believed that his love of learning was attributable to his birth mother, Nancy Hanks, who died when he was nine years old, it was actually his stepmother, Sarah Bush Johnston, who he called his "angel mother." Lincoln didn't hesitate to admit that his two mothers were responsible for his becoming, according to many historians, the greatest US president in history.

Leadership in a man is often considered a paramount trait for success, but there are many ways for a man to attain recognition. Two men whose names are instantly recognizable because of their innovations have lavishly credited their mothers for the achievements in their lives.

Thomas Edison's mother, Nancy, refused to give up on him when teachers labeled him as being addled and unable to learn. Instead, she home-schooled him, and because of her efforts, Thomas went on to greatness, inventing the incandescent light bulb, the phonograph, and the motion picture camera. He was credited with 1,093 US patents in his name. It appears that the standard used to measure intelligence in the nineteenth century wasn't always accurate in its predictions. Edison recognized the importance of his mother in his development. He said about her, "My mother was the making of me. She was so true, so sure of me; and I felt I had something to live for, someone I must not disappoint" (Deseret, 2006).

Alexander Graham Bell's mother, Eliza Grace Symonds Bell, was partially deaf, and yet she played the piano well. Alexander was deeply affected by his mother's loss of hearing and learned manual finger language that enabled him to speak with her. He was home-schooled until he attended high school. Although he wasn't a top student when it came to the usual academic subject matter, he had a curious mind and a unique ability for problem solving. At the age of twelve, he invented a machine to husk wheat. But his passion, in his efforts to help the deaf, was always focused on the transmission of sound. Bell's mother's perseverance in dealing with her hearing loss inspired her son to study hearing and eventually patent the first practical telephone.

Many of the men who were influenced by their mother allude to these woman as being saintly. Perhaps the idiom "like mother like son" is most aptly used to illustrate the spirituality of Mahatma Gandhi and his mother, Putilbai, who took the practice of her religion seriously. She went daily to the temple, and on Chaturmas, a fasting day similar to Lent, she would take the extra step and occasionally set up additional requirements for herself. Gandhi recounted the time that she vowed not to have food without seeing the sun. This was a major commitment, as it was the rainy season. It's easy to see that Gandhi's mother was his model of spirituality in the three promises that he made to her. He vowed that he would never eat flesh, drink alcohol, and would look upon other women as his mother or sister. He speaks of learning from his mother the importance of sacrificing oneself for another and says of her in his autobiography *The Story of My Experiments with Truth*, "The outstanding impression that my mother has left on my memory is saintliness" (Deseret, 2006).

AT THIS POINT, we should acknowledge the fact that not all mothers exert a good influence on their sons, and that some women could never be called "saintly." Catherine de Medici is an example of a woman with very few motherly qualities. She was Queen of France in the sixteenth century and had three sons whom she controlled with an iron fist. At first glance, it might appear that she unselfishly took certain actions to help her sons stay in power. However, many accounts of her behavior indicate that she was more focused on her own interests, and her behavior was solely motivated to enhance her power. The years that her sons reigned were known as the age of Catherine de Medici. This appellation underscores her prominence during this time, even though some of her rulings on behalf of her sons resulted in horrendous outcomes. A case in point is the St. Bartholomew's Day Massacre, which resulted in the death of thousands of Huguenots. It's a sure bet that these Huguenots would have fared better if de Medici had less of an influence on the lives of her sons. Perhaps you might be thinking that it was only in past eras that the greatest influence on a man's life was his mother, but you'll soon see that your assumption is false.

TODAY

I would be remiss not to mention examples of other women who have influenced men. In America, F. Scott Fitzgerald was considered a literary great. Almost as famous as Fitzgerald was his wife, Zelda. Much of the content of his writings, such as *The Great Gatsby*, was based on his wife's persona, especially his depictions of flappers. Zelda wasn't the only wife who made an impact on her husband's career. According to the Walt Disney Family Museum, we can thank Lillian, Walt Disney's wife, for Mickey Mouse not being named Mortimer Mouse. Walt made sure to consult her for approval of his ideas, and evidently, his dream of a Mortimer Mouse didn't pass muster with Lilian. Cesar Chavez was a well-known civil rights activist who founded the first farm workers union in America. However, the name of Dolores Huerta was less recognized, and yet she was Chavez's "right hand" and cofounded the National Farm Workers Association with him. Although we can hunt for additional examples of a wife, daughter, lover, or female boss's influence on a man, there are an overwhelming number of examples of a mom being a man's major influence that keep popping up, and that compel us to focus on these stories.

Perhaps the most succinct summary of a mother's importance in a son's life is captured in the Italian song "Mamma," written in 1940 by Cesare Andrea Bixio. If you have never heard it, then it's time to grab a few tissues and download the version sung by Luciano Pavarotti or Andrea Bocelli. The lyrics, ". . . my most beautiful song is you . . . you are life . . ." leave no doubt that, at least to an Italian man, Mamma holds the most important place in their heart. According to the 2021 American Community Survey, almost sixteen million people identify themselves as Italian American. If about half of them are men, then that's a lot of momma's boys. But what about the enormous number of men in the world who aren't Italian or of Italian heritage? Here are a few non-Italians who were outspoken in identifying the woman who most influenced their lives.

A name that stands out in French history is Napoleon Bonaparte. He was the emperor of France and widely considered one of the greatest military leaders in history. Nonetheless, he was a bowl of mush when it came to his relationship with his mother. He is quoted as saying, "My success and everything good that I have done, I owe to my mother." He was of the old-school mentality that was convinced that men were superior to women. Consequently, attributing male virtues to a woman would be considered an ultimate form of praise. Napoleon unabashedly granted this highest form of tribute to his mother when he said, "Her tenderness was severe, here was the head of a man on the body of a woman." Apparently, the admiration was mutual as Napoleon's mother accompanied her son in his first exile to Elba. As a side note, it's interesting to reflect on the fact that although Napoleon's Napoleonic Code vastly improved men's rights in France, it had disastrous consequences on the status of women. Napoleon's attitude toward women, aside from his mother, is captured in his remark that, "The leading lady of the world is she who makes the most children." Nonetheless, Mommy was a major presence in Napoleon's life.

Prince William lost his mother, Princess Diana, at the age of fifteen. He insisted that the short time that they shared shaped his destiny.

There were reports that perhaps Diana and William were a bit too close, as she relied on him even when he was still very young, calling him her little old wise man. She would have him accompany her to interviews and business meetings, such as the one with Piers Morgan in 1996 when William was only thirteen. Diana even encouraged him to ask questions at these meetings. Conceivably, this type of interaction helped prepare William for the notoriety that would always be part of his life. In the 2017 HBO documentary *Diana, Our Mother, Her Life, and Legacy*, William talks about the death of his mother and the suffering he endured while his life crumbled with the whole world watching. He remarked that this suffering "gives me positivity and strength to know that I can face anything the world can throw at me." William was inspired by his mother even after she passed from this earth. His connection with her continues as he keeps her spirit alive for his children. In addition to displaying her photos in his home, he directs his three children annually to make cards for the grandmother whom they never met.

We also can find many men in modern politics who attribute their accomplishments to the influence of their mothers. Often, this influence is not the result of a direct relationship between parent and child but rather an outcome of circumstances. Barack Obama was the forty-fourth president of the United States. Obama's mother, Stanley Ann Dunham, was a free thinker who married a man from Kenya and gave birth to Obama when she was eighteen. She wanted adventure and traveled the world where she spoke out about poverty and racism. Obama's alcoholic father abandoned him when he was an infant, so the title of his book, *Dreams from My Father* is a little misleading. Dunham divorced Obama's birth father, remarried an Indonesian man, and moved with her son to Indonesia. Obama went to school in Jakarta for four years until he was ten years old. His mother believed that he was destined for greatness, and to attain that greatness, he needed a strong English-language education. She thought that he wouldn't be able to receive this education in Jakarta, so she sent him back to Hawaii to live with his grandparents. Although he spent much of his childhood with his grandparents, his mother instilled in him a thirst for education, social justice, and the importance of providing opportunities for others. She even foreshadowed one of her son's early jobs when she worked in community development in Java. Barrack spoke of her as a dominant figure in his formative years and acknowledged her great influence on his life in the preface to his book, stating, "What is best in me, I owe to her."

THE ACCUMULATION OF wealth is a major goal that both men and women hope to achieve. Therefore, it follows that tremendous praise might be heaped upon a person who can influence the financial success of a man. As of July 2024, Elon Musk was the wealthiest person in the world. Although his mom, Maye, says Elon didn't always follow her advice, especially on financial matters when he grew older, nonetheless, she became a role model for Elon. She was a single mom survivor of domestic abuse and worked full time to support her three children while getting two master's degrees. She subsequently became a supermodel, author, and finalist for the Miss South Africa Pageant. She was also responsible for keeping Elon's first software company, Zip2, up and running by overseeing the company's operations, as well as giving her entire savings of ten thousand dollars to the company to help with expenses. Although Maye never attained her son's wealth, she was no slouch. Her ambition and drive inspired Elon to do great things.

Most of us are not billionaires, generals, or biblical prophets, and yet we experience the same emotions in our relationships as people who are instantly recognizable. Now that we've heard about the rich and famous, let's find out how the typical contemporary male in our survey answered the question, "What woman influenced you most in your life, e.g., mom, wife, daughter, boss, teacher, authority figure, etc.?" Men's completed responses by percentage are as follows:

MEN'S RESPONSES

INFLUENCER	PERCENTAGE
Mom	57
Wife	13
Other (daughter, boss, teacher, grandmother, etc.)	30

Certain men's comments noted below in response to this question stand out because of their sensitivity:

- "Mom, she taught me what a wife and mother should be."
- "Mum brought me into this world, nurtured and gave me guidance."
- "My wife, inspired me to my best every day."
- "Mom. Originally my dad died when I was three. Mom never remarried or dated. Then, best friend until I was ten or so. She lived around the corner. We live on opposite sides of the country, but still talk, then wife, now my two daughters . . ."

Our female survey respondents were provided with a separate survey in which they guessed the men's answers to the above question. Here are the women's completed responses by percentage:

WOMEN'S RESPONSES

INFLUENCER	PERCENTAGE
Mom	84
Wife	5
Other (daughter, boss, teacher, grandmother etc.)	11

Surprisingly, the women's responses barely acknowledged the idea that any woman could influence a man as profoundly as his mother does. The women's responses in contrast to the men's were slightly sardonic as indicated in some of their comments.

- "I don't believe men are influenced by women."
- "They would say that it was their wife, but really it was their mom, grandma or older sister."
- "Depends on the person."
- "I'd like to say his daughter, but probably his mom."

Well, I think that it's almost unanimous that Mom is the winner, according to the responses of both the men and women survey participants. I don't know if it means that there are a lot of mama's boys out there, or simply that mothers put the fear of God in their sons, and therefore men know what the correct answer should be.

As much fun as it might be to attribute omnipotent powers of coercion to mothers, we need to discover the real reason why so many men identify their mothers as the greatest influence in their lives. *The Journal of Social Cognitive and Affective Neuroscience*, states that mothers experience "high self-overlap" when they picture their children in distressing situations. Brain imaging tests revealed that a mother's brain showed reactions to their children's distress as if they themselves were in danger. This bonded connectivity between mother and child likely produces total trust, thus enhancing a mother's ability to appropriately influence their child's life. A man's emotional attachment to his mother reflects in his relationships with others—for good or for bad. At the end of it all, we may claim that men are scientifically programmed to be most influenced by their mothers. And that should put a smile on all mothers' faces except perhaps the moms of our fictional characters, Jim, Buddy, and Noah, who, had they participated in the survey, would likely have chosen women other than their moms as the greatest influence in their lives.

We need to give a big thank you to all the men who have admitted that certain women have influenced them in their lives. However, a more daunting question now arises. Do men in their hearts truly believe that women and men are equal? We're about to find out in our next chapter.

CHAPTER 2

DO MEN THINK WOMEN ARE EQUAL? DEPENDS ON WHO'S PAYING FOR DINNER.

It's a Tuesday night and Jim, Buddy, and Noah are sitting again at their favorite table in their neighborhood bar. Although the men usually pick different topics each month, they've decided to continue discussing how they feel about women and the women in their lives. Not only are they learning more about each other but also are clarifying for themselves thoughts that they rarely examine about women.

Tonight's topic is women's equality with men, or more specifically, whether men think that women are their equals. Jim eagerly begins the conversation. "Throughout my life, I have believed that men and women are biologically designed to perform different roles in society. However, after my conversation with my daughter, I now understand that although anatomically a man's and woman's bodies may be better suited to accomplish specific tasks, women are entitled to the same state of equality as men, especially in status, rights, and opportunities."

Jim looks at his friends to see their reactions and then, hoping that it's safe to continue, says, "After observing my mother, sister, and wife's relationship with their children, I believe that many women have certain capabilities of nurturing that men often lack. I recall that after the birth of my first child, I felt incredible relief at the thought of returning to work. My wife experienced diametrically different emotions as she couldn't bear to let our child out of her sight, but her feelings might not be universal to all women. My daughter has told me that she might not want to include motherhood in her life's plan."

Jim now recognizes the significance of gender differences when it comes to raising a family. It seems an acceptable norm in society is that men may wish to have several offspring. But the expectation is that women stay home to raise the children, relinquishing their professional or personal goals. In fact, many think it's unnatural for men to be the primary caregivers for their children. Jim realizes that many people might harbor different, usually unspoken thoughts about a woman holding the same sentiments. Such a woman might be categorized as unmotherly, selfish, and lacking in feminine traits, when the reality is that she might simply be driven by other career motivators for self-actualization. Jim concludes by telling Buddy and Noah, "I'm finally able to let go of my preconceived notions that the home is a woman's place and instead view women as equal to, yet different from men."

Buddy is almost frothing at the mouth in his desire to speak. "Men are stronger than women who easily become victims of crime because they can't adequately defend themselves," says Buddy with a smirk. Noah laughs at Buddy as he recalls the wrestling matches that he has lost with his girlfriend. But Noah decides to remain silent, as Buddy rambles on why women are not equal to men. Buddy explains to Jim and Noah, "I know that you both sometimes think that I'm not intellectually equal to either of you, but I'm in a class of my own when it comes to sheer brawn and fearlessness. As a freight driver, I'm sometimes required to lift tremendously heavy things. I also occasionally must drive through the night for a timed delivery. You might be thinking that a woman could easily drive a truck, but I know that unless she's an Amazon, it's unlikely that she could lift some of the cargo that I've had to lift. Also, my truck has broken down many times on lonely back roads where sexual predators would love to find a woman alone in her vehicle. I stand by my words that women and men are unequal, as women are physiologically unfit to stand up against a man *mano a mano*. Hey, I'm not a complete idiot, as I'm the first to admit that there are some things, like nursing a baby, that only a woman can do. Each gender needs to accept that they're better at different things. Sure, I say, give women the opportunity to try out for the things that men do in the world, but they'll fail in the end. And, when they do, how constructive is that? They'll just feel worse." Evidently, Buddy prizes physical strength above all other human characteristics.

Noah has listened to Jim and Buddy and has decided to be transparent about his thoughts on the equality of women, even if it means exposing his own vulnerabilities. His opening words to Jim and Buddy are a little startling. "I think that women are superior to men in many respects. I have many female professor friends who are single mothers and have earned their doctorates while emotionally and financially supporting their children. They had to continue their studies and work assignments while their children slept, whereas my divorced male professor friends just had to remember to put their support checks in the mail for their children by a certain date, thereby fulfilling their court-ordered obligations as a parent."

Although Noah hates bringing up his infidelities with women, he continues. "Women professors also put their romantic lives on the back burner to focus on their families. I honestly don't know whether this simply points out that men have a stronger sex drive than women or that women are able to exert willpower better than men to avoid sexual temptations. I know only too well that there are many of these temptations in a university setting for singles of both sexes, and yet my women friends refuse to cross that line, something that I didn't have the strength of character to resist. My conclusion is that men and women aren't equal. There are many matters in which women are biologically predisposed to excel over men. However, although I never thought that I'd agree with Buddy on the subject of a woman's equality, it's indisputable that men, in general terms, are physically stronger than women. This reality affects their competence in a number of ways. As an example, competitive skills in certain sports rely on a person's strength. Likewise, strength comes into play when it comes to self-defense. Women must fight for the opportunities that society deems an entitlement for men. Women will never be equal to men in all things until society refuses to accept that there is physical gender bias."

The three friends each concede that men and women are different. However, only Noah affirms that a woman's differences have a positive impact on society. Next up, we'll learn more about this matter when we delve into men's attitudes from the past.

YESTERDAY

If the Bible says it's so then we better believe it's true, or so they say. Unfortunately, much of the Bible contradicts itself. One way of dealing with this confusion is to follow whatever version of the truth makes you happiest. In the case of women's equality, I defer to the words of Genesis 2-27-28 in the New Revised Standard Version of the Catholic Bible that states, "So God created man in his own image, in the image of God he created him; male and female he created them. God blessed them and told them to be "fruitful and increase in number; fill the earth and subdue it. Rule over the fish of the sea and the birds of the air and over every living creature that moves on the ground." My take on this mandate is that, as God is speaking to *"them,"* it can be said that God gave the power to rule the earth equally to both men and women, and who wants to argue with God after seeing what happened to Adam and Eve. Although it seems this decree clearly established the equality of women, history reveals that the status of women was far from equal to that of men, and that some men would rather face the wrath of God than give up their perceived privileges.

The King James Version of the Bible tells us that the Levite believed that his concubine was his property, therefore he felt justified in giving her to a group of men who raped and abused her throughout the night. This might explain the subsequent female aggression recounted in the Bible during the time of the Levite. A woman like Deborah became a charismatic military leader to demonstrate that she wouldn't just lie down and be subjugated to abuse because she was a woman. Instead, she played a prominent role in Israel's capture of the lands of Canaan. Her accomplishments showed future generations that not all women had to take subordinate roles to men.

The story of Lydia in the Bible illustrates how it was possible for a woman to achieve power, even if she didn't want to engage in battles. Purple cloth was associated with royalty and status, and most merchants selling it were very successful financially, including Lydia. She also became known as the first documented convert to Christianity in Europe. She may have not been seen as equal by the men in her world, but her financial prosperity provided her with certain liberties not available to most women in her day.

Ostensibly, when life and death are at stake, there is no question that women are valued equally with men. Studies such as the one in *Science* magazine (May 15, 2015) indicate that equality between men and women occurred in hunter-gatherer tribes. The very survival of the tribe depended on egalitarianism. Archaeologists have discovered tombs containing women buried with hunting tools. Children were cared for by the entire tribe in a real-life adherence to the "it takes a village" philosophy. This freed women to hunt side by side with men. However, it remains to be seen if today's modern woman would appreciate the opportunity to engage in life-threatening endeavors to establish her equality with men.

Aristotle best summed up society's attitude about the status of women from the fourth through eighth centuries in Greece. "Women were doomed to be subservient to men because they were unable to . . . control themselves physically and psychologically through the exercise of reason the way men can" (Whaley, 16). However, practicality sometimes demanded that the men of Greece admit that women were useful. For instance, Greek agriculture was crucial to the community, and female fertility goddesses such as Demeter and Persephone were not considered just equal to men but also venerated.

The Greeks also appreciated a sharp mind, and some women

were valued for their intellect. Hypatia was the leader of the Neoplatonist school of philosophy in Alexandria. She was a renowned mathematician, philosopher, astronomer, and teacher. Many prominent men were her pupils and acknowledged that in many ways she was superior. Socrates of Constantinople describes her as someone "who made such attainments in literature and science, as to far surpass all the philosophers of her own time."

On the other hand, as recounted in stories of Greek male heroes, women like Medea and the deadly Sirens were portrayed as evil beings who existed solely to disrupt men's lives. It's plausible to believe that the negative message contained in these tales affected men's attitudes toward accepting women as equals. Unlike these fantasy figures, all flesh-and-blood Greek women were powerless and expected to marry and find satisfaction in taking care of their husbands and family. Once married, a Greek woman would always be known as simply the wife of a Greek citizen, without any rights of her own.

The ancient Romans shared the Greeks' disdain for the rights of women. Roman women were obliged to nominate a family member to act in their interests in all matters. They were prohibited from receiving an education, and although they oversaw the upbringing of their children, in the event of a divorce the children legally belonged to the father. Emperor Augustus captured the thoughts of men regarding women in Roman times with his words, "Nature has made it so that we cannot live with them particularly comfortably, but we can't live without them at all." Surprisingly, these words have endured even today.

Men still can be heard jokingly uttering Augustus's words, but of course not usually in the company of women. Although few Roman women fought back against their preordained roles and led great armies like Deborah, there were some women whose accomplishments stood out during this male-dominated era.

Agrippina, wife of emperor Claudius and mother of Nero, decided to follow an unusual path to power and equality. She murdered her husband and publicly announced that she was taking over as emperor until her teenage son could assume power. Although male Romans were outraged, she persevered in her demands for equality.

It is evident on the coins from this era that Agrippina and Nero held equal power as both of their faces are equally sized and depicted on the coins. Few Roman women possessed the fortitude to claim their rights like Agrippina but instead relied on their husbands to establish their status in the world.

Julia Soaemias is a little-known name in Roman history. She was a wealthy woman who was able to pay for a rebellion against the emperor so that her son, Elagabalus, also known as Marcus Aurelius Antoninus, could ascend to the position. The reality was that even though her son appeared to be the leader, she was so powerful that she became the first woman to be allowed into the Roman Senate. Unfortunately, her equal rights were short-lived, as her son angered the Senate with his ineptitude. He devalued the currency, worshipped foreign gods, took male lovers, and married a Vestal Virgin, who were considered powerful priestesses at the time. Roman subjects agreed that it was time for him to go. The military guard carried out the people's wishes by assassinating him and Julia. At least you could say that the Romans distributed their punishments equivalently to men and women. Thankfully, women in the future won't have to fear for their lives in exchange for equality.

Because of the royal laws of succession, when her father Prince Edward died and there was no other legitimate issue in the royal line, Queen Victoria assumed her role as England's monarch. It would seem that having a woman leader would have resulted in a total acceptance of women's equality. However, England remained a patriarchy, and even Victoria had to abide by strict social conventions not applicable to men. Even though she was queen, she was an unmarried woman, and this meant that she had to live with her mother until she married. The queen had private tutors who gave her a superior education in the classics. This contrasted sharply with the average woman's education, which was limited to her becoming an "angel of the home," which meant that she should be well versed in painting, singing, music, and dancing. Women had no rights to sue, vote, or own property. If she married well, a woman would be on a pedestal; for those less fortunate, their jobs would be as domestic servants.

Strangely enough, even though Queen Victoria wielded vast amounts of power, she was no proponent of equal rights for women as is obvious in her letter to the King of Prussia. Her words, "The Queen is most anxious to enlist everyone who can speak or write to join in checking this mad, wicked folly of 'Woman's Rights,' with all its attendant horrors, on which her poor feeble sex is bent, forgetting every sense of womanly feeling and propriety," was an outrageous assault against women's equality. It seems that Queen Victoria either forgot that she was a woman or felt threatened at the thought of other women attaining some of the freedoms that she possessed. Obviously, men of the Victorian era were comfortable with the balance of power remaining in their hands since it was sanctioned by their ruler.

Victoria probably would have applauded the Japanese for their description of a woman's role in society. They believed that "The Japanese maiden, as pure as the purest Christian virgin, will at the command of her father enter the brothel tomorrow, and prostitute herself for life" (Griffis, The Mikado's Empire). Wow, that just about says it all about the rights of women in Japan in the nineteenth century. Although this seems like a bleak blow to women's rights the words "prostitute herself for life" in Japan can be interpreted to mean something other than someone getting paid for sex. Many Japanese women married and became housewives and subverted their opportunities for equality in exchange for the protections given to married women. The motto for Japanese women became to be "good wives and wise mothers." To contemporary women, this might not seem like that much of a step up from being a paid sex worker. However, in exchange for running a household, men worked and handed their paychecks over to their wives. Being a good wife and mother didn't sound too bad to Japanese women in the nineteenth century, considering that prostitution was one of the few alternative ways for a woman to have food and shelter other than through marriage.

TODAY

By the beginning of the twentieth century women activists in Japan, such as Raicho Hiratsuka, were starting to make their voices for equality heard. Hiratsuka founded the New Women's Association, which was responsible for overturning a law that had barred women from joining political organizations and holding or attending political meetings. However, although there were some activists like Hiratsuka who fought for women's rights, the general consensus was that these women were turning their backs on their feminine side.

During World War 1, women assumed important roles in the workplace as they replaced the men who went off to fight. Unfortunately, their contributions were quickly forgotten after the war ended, and they were again exhorted to return to domestic roles. The New York Labor Federation officially expressed this sentiment in their statement, "The same patriotism, which induced women to enter industry during the war, should induce them to vacate their positions after the war." This exhortation to take a step back from their newly found economic autonomy wasn't appreciated by women who had experienced a small taste of freedom and equality and wanted more. Their yearning was exemplified in the social changes noted in the Roaring Twenties, particularly in the appearance of the flapper, who had short hair, smoked cigarettes, and exhibited a sensuality not generally practiced by the average woman of the times. Women of this era saw that they had a right to certain freedoms and were starting to make their voices heard.

Although flappers flaunted their flamboyant behavior, there was still widespread resistance to the concept of women's equality. It was thought that the passage of the 19th Amendment in America, giving women the right to vote, would help equalize the rights of men and women. However, even the media had a hard time accepting this egalitarianism and were quick to quantify it. *The New York Times* published an editorial about women having the right to vote. They conceded that mature females might now be able to engage in the political process, but the "scantily clad, jazzing flapper to whom a dance, a new hat, or a man with a car is of more importance than the fate of nations should not be permitted to vote."

It wasn't only American women who were making their marks in the world during the twentieth century. Mary Bailey, an Anglo-Irish aviator who was considered a pioneer of Aeronautics, showed that she could match a man's achievements and even surpass them when she flew her plane from London to Cape Town, South Africa, and back. At the time, this was the longest solo flight accomplished by anyone.

Many other milestones advancing women's equality were established in the twentieth century. In addition to the 19th Amendment, Margaret Sanger opened the first birth-control clinic. The walls limiting a woman's opportunities were being razed, and yet men of that generation failed to fall into line with this new definition of gender roles. DH Lawrence, among other influential thinkers of the time, declared that women who abandoned their traditional submissive gender roles were causing "the decline of the West."

Writers frequently reflect the values of the times in their writings. A good indication of the ambivalence of men regarding the emerging female freedoms of the twentieth century are evident in the writings of many writers such, as F. Scott Fitzgerald who is credited with popularizing the flapper. Speaking about his depiction of this *new* woman, he clarifies that she represents not only freedom, but also social disorder and lack of direction. In a letter, he stated, "If I had anything to do with creating the manners of the modern American girl, I certainly made a botch of the job" (Life in Letters, 110). Women may have been dancing in the streets, but men were still hoping that they'd return to their homes and get dinner on the table.

THE 1950S WERE a time of confusion in a woman's quest for equality. The dreams of many men came to fruition as women returned home. Domesticity was lauded in the media with shows like *Leave It to Beaver* and *Father Knows Best*, setting the tone for expectations for women. *I Love Lucy* mirrored the attitude of many men regarding women in the workplace. Lucy was portrayed as a ditsy redhead who couldn't be taken seriously. Lucy failed at every job she tried when she went to work outside the home. During this time, sex before marriage was taboo, and courses like home economics were taught to girls in school to prepare them to assume their roles as homemakers.

Even though gender equality was guaranteed in the Universal Declaration of Human Rights that was adopted by the UN General Assembly in 1948, women in the 1950s couldn't enter into contracts, buy or sell property, or hold office. Legal incentives to balance the equality between men and women were being ignored. Birth control pills were first manufactured in 1960, and it wasn't until the late 1960s and early 1970s that women started to see real changes in their status, but even then, their parity with men wasn't universally accepted.

In 1963, Congress passed the Equal Pay Act, the first federal law against gender discrimination. Women's legal rights were further promoted by the Civil Rights Act of 1964, which banned employment discrimination based on gender and race. However, many men, including President John F. Kennedy, still saw women as second-class citizens. In a televised discussion in 1962, he said, "We want to be sure that women are used as effectively as they can to provide a better life for our people, in addition to meeting their primary responsibility, which is in the home." It's interesting to note Kennedy's choice of words, "be sure that women are used effectively." These words suggest that women are implements rather than autonomous people. Kennedy wasn't the only one who wanted things to go back to what they were in the good old days.

Betty Friedan and Gloria Steinem were some of the early proponents of gender equality. Friedan founded the National

Organization for Women, and Steinem was the co-founder of the National Women's Political Caucus and the Women's Action Alliance. They both worked tirelessly to raise awareness about gender discrimination. Nevertheless, a woman still couldn't get a credit card without her husband's signature, and Yale and Princeton didn't accept female undergraduate students until 1969; Harvard waited until 1977 when it merged with Radcliffe College. Even though feminism was becoming a force to be reckoned with, the courts continued to hold women back. In 1961, the US Supreme Court unanimously upheld a Florida law that exempted women from serving on juries. At the time, the court consisted of all-male justices. This was another demoralizing indication of men's attitudes toward women's equality in the early 1960s.

THE TWENTY-FIRST CENTURY was filled with innovative ideas. Artificial intelligence was no longer something that only existed in films. You could use 3D printing to create your own toys. Online streaming threatened to make cable television and movie theaters extinct. Nonetheless, the search for equality for women has been a story of ups and downs.

The MeToo movement struck fear into the hearts of sexual predators as women cried out against sexual abuse, harassment, and the rape culture. While women have surpassed men in the amount of education attained, there has been nothing like convergence in the fields of study in which men and women get degrees. The pay gap still exists. Women have broken the glass ceiling in many professions, and yet only six countries give women equal legal work rights as men. Even companies that market to the next generation of women show little sensitivity by promoting demeaning female stereotypes. At one time, Gymboree sold T-shirts that said, *Smart like Daddy* for the boys and *Pretty like Mommy* for the girls; this was in 2016—not 1950.

We still have a long way to go on the road to equality, and unfortunately, there are countries where women may never be considered equal to men. The Taliban has mastered in the art of violating the human rights of women. This Islamic fundamentalist and jihadist political movement in Afghanistan dictates what women must wear, how they should travel, and even what kind of cell phones females may have. Girls are banned from secondary and higher education, and in 1996 it was decreed that all women should be banned from employment. The most recent atrocity occurred in August 2024 when the Taliban issued a degree prohibiting women from speaking or showing their faces in public. But we don't have to travel to an obscure part of the world to find such suppression of women as we can discern similar feelings in leaders of established societies.

In April 2013, there was excitement among Japanese women when the longest serving Japanese Prime Minister Shinzo Abe announced his groundbreaking policy of "Womenomics." However, this excitement was short-lived when it became apparent that nothing much would change for women in Japan. As so often happens, politicians say what they think people want to hear but rarely follow up their promises with action.

Abe promised that the employment rate would go up for women and it did, but these jobs were part-time or contract positions, while only 12 percent of corporate management jobs went to women. Despite his rhetoric, Abe continued to emphasize the importance of male succession. This practice ensured the impossibility of a woman becoming emperor. Abe also rejected the accusations that the Japanese army was involved in the recruitment of *comfort (sex slaves) women during World War II*. Japan had a long way to go to establish women's equality with men. In 2021, according to the World Economic Forum, Japan is in 120th place out of 153 countries with a gender equity gap of 34.4 percent. Honoring the family and being a breadwinner are still considered male domain.

"When people push boundaries too far, it's not because they are strong but because they are weak, but maybe weakness is not the worst quality for a woman." With these words, the leader of Russia, Vladimir Putin, doesn't hesitate to declare his disinterest in women achieving their rights. And sad to say that even in the United States, the 45th and 47th president, Donald Trump, has openly displayed condescension, some might even say contempt, for women's abilities. During an interview with a female reporter in 2014, Trump said, "I mean, we could say politically correct, that look doesn't matter, but the look obviously matters. Like, you wouldn't have your job if you weren't beautiful." Even in Trump's poor grammar, his words unabashedly show he was more interested in a woman's appearance than her abilities. The words of these world leaders cement the reality that many influential men still believe that women should remain subordinate to men.

Notwithstanding what some world leaders have said, there's hope that not all heads of government think that women are being undeserved when it comes to equal rights. Justin Trudeau, the Canadian Prime Minister, immediately after he was elected, took a bold step to promote women's equality by making sure that at least half of his cabinet were women. When Joe Biden took office after defeating Trump in 2020, he nominated a record twelve women to the twenty-six cabinet-level jobs in his administration—not including his female vice president, Kamala Harris. Biden recognized that for all women to work for parity with men, to effect real change we need to have women in the type of powerful positions that enable them to mandate policies that will ensure women's rights. Mr. Trudeau has initiated that process for Canadian women and Biden made strides toward it.

———

BEFORE we go to the results of our surveys, I want to touch on something that appears too strange to be real. In 2022, the state of

New Jersey filed a civil rights complaint against Pine Valley Golf Club in New Jersey for gender discrimination. This 108-year-old club didn't try to hide its belief that women are unequal to men. Until April 2021, women couldn't become members and, with narrow exceptions, couldn't play golf or access the facilities. Women also were prohibited from owning any of the nineteen houses on the property. The Pine Valley Golf Club had gotten away with this discrimination because they had declared that they were a *private club*, and private clubs could do anything they wanted. The state disagreed that the club was private as it was intertwined with the borough of Pine Valley. All of the land in the borough was owned by the club, so the club actually was the borough. It would have probably made the members of the club happy if they could have placed a sign on the property that said, *WOMEN STAY OUT.* Acting New Jersey Attorney General Matthew Platkin made it clear that not all men in the state were like the members of Pine Valley Golf Club. He firmly stated that "gender-based discrimination has no place in New Jersey, period." Cheers to Mr. Platkin.

Although in the twenty-first century, it's socially frowned upon for a man to claim that a woman's place is still in the home, clearly there are still men who wish they could be transported back to the 1950s. It's interesting to note that even religious institutions seemingly support this subordinate rank of women in their leadership structures. According to a Pew Research Center report, as of 2012, only 11 percent of the largest congregations in America were led by women. Roman Catholics, Southern Baptists, Mormons, and the Orthodox Church do not ordain women. Evidently, the philosophy of these religions rejects the dictates of the section of the Bible containing Genesis, in which power is equally distributed between men and women.

It's now time to share with you what the survey respondents of both surveys think about women's equality with men. The *yes* answers are very straightforward and don't produce any extra comments. However, many of the *no* responses were accompanied by additional remarks, some of which might make you chuckle or put your fist through a wall. Some of these additional comments will be noted beneath the applicable chart. Men's responses by percentages to the question, "Do you believe that women are innately equal to men in all characteristics, e.g., intellect, emotions, ambitions, leadership potential?" are as follows:

MEN'S RESPONSES

RESPONSES	PERCENTAGE
Yes	76
No	23
Other	1

Although our male survey respondents overwhelmingly declared their belief in the equality of women, the survey provided us with some interesting comments from male respondents who obviously don't support women's rights. Let's take a look:

- "Women are emotionally driven which impairs their ability to lead."
- "Statistically speaking, men are more advanced in leadership qualities. That's simply a simple fact."
- "Women have less muscle mass."
- "Men are willing to take risks, women are more cautious."
- "God, I hope not!"
- "No! If we were equal the world would be in crisis."

Well, at least our last respondent softened the blow by admitting that the world needs women in some capacity, even if he didn't think that they were equal to men. The women's survey results show a startling contrast between the women respondents' perceptions of the men's answers and the actual male respondents' answers:

WOMEN'S RESPONSES

RESPONSES	PERCENTAGE
Yes	21
No	67
Other	12

It's fascinating to note that only 21 percent of women respondents thought that men would answer affirmatively to the question of whether women were equal to men, while 76 percent of the men's answers were *yes* to this question. It appears that a woman's life experience influences her attitude regarding gender equality. The large disparity between the percentages in the two surveys indicates that our female respondents might admonish a man to think about the oxymoron of *Do as I do, not as I say.*"

Many female respondents note that a big component in a man's consideration of gender equality depends on considering a woman's emotional state. Here are a few of the women's comments."

- "I think that most men have implicit bias against women and think that women are more emotional or irrational than men."
- "Men know for a fact that they are stronger and more 'alpha' than all women in general."
- "Many men subconsciously find women to be inferior intellectually and with respect to leadership."
- "I think that most men are selfish and only view women in terms of how they benefit men."
- "Men say women are too emotional because men have never learned to properly express their emotions."

And to save the best for last, a female respondent says what she thinks a man would respond to the question, "What ways women are unequal to men?":

- "In every single way, except that we both breathe air."

It looks like women don't quite believe that men think women are equal to them. Despite the overwhelming percentage of men who claim that they believe that women and men are equal, women are skeptical of the authenticity of the men's responses.

—

JIM AND NOAH might lead us to believe that they think women are superior to men in many ways, but on the other hand, Buddy's attitude reinforces women's pessimism about men seeing women as equals. Women might need a little convincing that men admire and respect them as equals and a good beginning is an interchange of affection. Perhaps a little romance could be thrown into the mix. But do men understand a woman's concept of romance? Join me in the next chapter to find the answer.

CHAPTER 3

ROSES ARE RED, VIOLETS ARE BLUE, BUT WHAT THE HECK IS ROMANCE? I WISH THAT I KNEW.

It doesn't necessarily mean that you're not a romantic if finding a trail of rosebuds leading to your bed just makes you wonder how long it will take for you to clean up the mess. Or it doesn't make you a cynic if you think that the scene in the movie *The Notebook*, where the two characters are walking home from their first date and start to dance in the middle of the street, is goofy. However, if your partner's heart beats a little faster contemplating these scenarios, then you better be able to discern whether their reaction is the result of a pending heart attack, or that something about these events turns them on.

Jim, Buddy, and Noah settle in at their usual table at the bar and decide to tackle the sometimes-uncomfortable topic of romance, and how it is defined. Perhaps they're a bit leery of expressing the depth of their emotions for fear of looking unmanly. But they agree to be as honest as possible in their conversation.

Birthdays and holidays have always been celebrated robustly in Jim's childhood home. His wife's family, however, thought it was ridiculous to make a fuss over gift-giving. At Christmas, each child was given a department store shopping bag containing unwrapped practical gifts. Jim's wife swore that when she was married, all special occasions would be exciting, and gifts would be something memorable. She expected her gifts from Jim to be nothing less than awe-inspiring.

Jim, on the other hand, remembered the many hours his parents spent creating the Christmas wonderland of his youth. Now that much of the work would land on his shoulders, he was more in tune with the gift-giving habits of his wife's family. At any rate, he wanted to do whatever would make his wife the happiest.

When Jim told Buddy and Noah about a recent celebration of his wife's birthday, it became quickly obvious that he might not understand what his wife thought was a good gift. "I thought that I would make my wife happy with my choice of her gift this year. She constantly complained about how difficult it was to keep her cooking pot clean. I researched the best pot on the market and then spent three hundred dollars to buy her this super pot. Instead of beaming with joy over her gift, she looked at me with daggers in her eyes and told me that it was clear that I no longer considered her attractive. I thought that she had finally gone insane. My daughter again came to the rescue by taking me aside and explaining to me that no matter how long a woman and man have been together, a woman still wants to be treated as a man's desirable love interest, and that means pots were out as gifts." She said, "No woman wants to be desired just because she makes great chicken soup. Maybe your next gift to Mom should be perfume, earrings, a negligee, a spa day, or something a little less practical."

Jim realized that his friends might have a problem equating gifts with a woman's desirability. He knew that he had to somehow make the idea relatable with something that a man could understand. He asked Buddy and Noah a question: "As a man's virility is often associated with his sexual prowess, don't we all like to think that our partners consider us to be virile?" He reminded them that, "We don't appreciate mention of any inadequacies in that part of our lives and keeping this in mind, receiving a gift book on how to turn your partner on sexually would probably bruise our ego and be rejected. A woman feels this way when her partner ignores her sexuality by gifting her with household goods. Everyone has an image of themselves that they hope is projected into the world. I now know that my gifts to my wife should reflect my view of her as my partner in an intimate relationship, not that of a scullery maid in my home. She wants romance, and I guess the pot just didn't do it."

Pots, scullery maids . . . Buddy had no idea what Jim was talking about. Buddy said to his friends, "You both need to understand that a woman wants a man to take charge and not be at her mercy for every little thing that he does or doesn't do. I've always taken the lead in my relationships and there's been no complaints in what you call the *romance* department. When it comes right down to it, romance is a gussied-up word for sex. All the perfume in the world is no substitute for knowing how to make a woman moan with sexual satisfaction."

Jim and Noah cleared their throats at their friend's pearls of chauvinistic wisdom, a self-absorbed modern-day Romeo. Buddy continued. "The smoldering gazes, hand holding, and neck nibbling are all just preludes to the main act. When I want to take my date out for a romantic evening, I take her to my favorite bar and let her know that she can have as many beers as she wants. I know that it sounds like I'm being extravagant, but that's just the kind of guy that I am. Also, there's a side benefit to my generosity. After several beers, my date tends to be more amorous and eager to end the night at my apartment to engage in some romance." Let's hope that Buddy is able to continue meeting female versions of himself who like his slam, bam, thank you ma'am version of romance, otherwise, someday, he may be destined to live a lonely life.

It's easy to envision Noah sitting by a lake reading the famous British poet Lord Byron's words to his girlfriend: "She walks in beauty like the night, of cloudless climes and starry skies; And all that's best of dark and bright, Meet in her aspect and her eyes." Like Byron, Noah considers himself "an idealized but flawed character, capable of great passion" and because of this starry-eyed vision of himself, Noah feels secure that he knows the meaning of romance. He tells Jim and Buddy, "I typically leave little love notes on my girlfriend's pillow before I go to work, and I make sure to tell her how beautiful she is at least once a day. My idea of a casual date might seem over-the-top and a waste of energy if I'm using Buddy's idea of romance as a model. I usually pick an intimate neighborhood restaurant. I'll call the restaurant in advance to ask them to put flowers, a candle, and a special bottle of wine on the table. I don't consider myself a particularly handsome man, but I make sure that I'm always well-groomed, and if my girlfriend likes me in jeans and a T-shirt then that's what I'll wear around her. It's the little things that create a sense of romance. I must admit that I also get a kick out of the dreamlike atmosphere that my efforts create. I've been very successful in the past attracting women and maintaining relationships, so I must have hit the nail on the head in the romance department."

Although Jim, Buddy, and Noah might think they know the meaning of romance, the men of the Old Testament might be able to teach them a few tricks for using romance to make a woman happy.

YESTERDAY

Even as the "Song of Solomon" begins, it starts with romance. Solomon's bride gushes, "Let him kiss me with the kisses of his mouth! For your love is better than wine" (Song 1:2). Solomon recognizes the need for flattery in his response to his lover saying she is "The most beautiful among women" (Song1:8). This is a bride and groom who understand how to use effusive flattery to enhance their relationship, but they still have a long way to go to match the romance in the tale of Jacob and Rachel.

The story of Jacob and Rachel in Genesis underscores a rarefied type of romantic love. Jacob is so captivated by Rachel that he tells her father that he will work for seven years just to have her, and that's what he does. Unfortunately, Rachel's father is desperate to get rid of Rachel's older sister Leah. He tricks Jacob by bringing Leah to Jacob in the middle of the night, and before you know it the marriage is consummated. Jacob is then stuck with Leah. But Jacob is on fire with his love for Rachel and makes another momentous romantic act by offering seven more years of work in exchange for having Rachel. Jacob did fourteen years of servitude to have the love of his life. Most women would say that's romance.

A well-known example of romantic love in the Middle Ages is the tale of King Arthur, Queen Guinevere, and the knight Lancelot. Guinevere had affection for her husband Arthur, but her heart belonged to Lancelot. Although Camelot was just a fictional place with imagined characters, the image of a knight in shining armor on a white horse epitomizes every woman's dream of the perfect male. But we don't need to rely on fictional stories to find an illustration of romance in the Middle Ages. Perhaps the ultimate expression of romance during this time may be found in the writings of the renowned poet Dante Alighieri. Many would say Dante illustrated one of the greatest romantic gestures of all time, although, to some, his behavior might seem a little odd. Let's see what you think.

MOST PEOPLE, ASIDE from English Lit majors, probably haven't read Dante's three-part epic poem the "Divine Comedy" containing the Inferno, yet scholars consider this epic poem culturally important as one of the best works of Western Civilization. Interestingly, today Dante's Inferno is known to gamers as an exciting game for PlayStation and Xbox.

Writers often dedicate their work to special people in their lives. In Dante Alighieri's case, he dedicated his masterpiece to Beatrice, a woman whom he met just twice in his life, once when he was only nine years old. It was likely that Beatrice was unaware of Dante's love for her, but it didn't diminish his all-consuming passion. His love didn't involve lust or physicality that sometimes wanes over time, enabling it to burn brightly, even though it was unrequited. Perhaps part of the continuing allure could be attributed to the unattainability of the relationship. Upon meeting Beatrice for the second time at the age of eighteen, Dante expressed his adoration for her in his words, "She greeted me; and such was the virtue of her greeting that I seemed to experience the height of bliss." It didn't take much to make Dante happy. He continued to show adoration for her throughout the "Divine Comedy." Beatrice was portrayed as Dante's muse who interceded for him in the Inferno, represented his purpose in Purgatorio, and guided him through Paradiso. Depending on your viewpoint, this type of love might be called obsession or the ultimate expression of romantic love. Then again, I bet that his wife's heart didn't beat with joy when she thought about her husband's grand passion for another woman. Dante effectively showed that the written word could convey romance.

Several centuries later, the works of William Shakespeare captured the concept of tragedy in a romantic relationship in his play, *Romeo and Juliet*. The play was based on two real-life lovers in Verona Italy who gave up their lives for one another. This theme was used by Shakespeare as an example of the ultimate romantic sacrifice, which fortunately never caught on in the modern day.

———

IT WASN'T ONLY men who expressed their amorous feelings through writing. Elizabeth Barrett Browning penned many sonnets, including the famous "How Do I Love Thee, Let Me Count the Ways" as a love poem to her husband, Robert, during their courtship. In many English classes, her *Sonnets from the Portuguese* is used to illustrate the yearnings of romantic love. Many people don't realize that the word *Portuguese* in the title was an affectionate nickname given to Elizabeth by her husband. Elizabeth and Robert's courtship exemplified the attraction of forbidden fruit. Elizabeth's father hated Robert because he thought that he was a fortune hunter. He forbid his daughter to have anything to do with Robert. Elizabeth's response was to conduct her courtship secretly. In 1846, Elizabeth and Robert eloped and fled to Italy. He never saw her father again. Drama, strife, secrecy, tragedy, and passion; their love had all of the ingredients to make a person swoon.

Everyday couples in the nineteenth century demonstrated that they, too, understood the magic of language despite not being poets or playwrights. Not only did the Victorians excel at writing, but they also believed in love at first sight and no longer saw marriage as strictly a political or economic necessity. The Victorians wanted to marry for love and had companionate bonding. They wholeheartedly threw themselves into the trappings of courting and not only wrote letters to their loved ones but also kept diaries recording their courtships. Sentimental gifts were exchanged. Engagement rings, locks of hair, and pictures were all representations of romantic love. These tokens were unheard of in earlier centuries when relationships were entered into to unify powerful families or expand one's financial status. Victorian men and women now looked for ways to make their lover's hearts beat faster.

ALTHOUGH IN TODAY'S world it might seem the opposite of romance, in the nineteenth century, matrimonial advertisements were also taken out to note what a person needed in a mate. This new freedom to pick one's mate encouraged people to become very choosy. However, men and women couldn't cavalierly behave recklessly. Couples had to adhere to strict rules of etiquette to be followed when engaging in courtship. There were even guidelines that stated the correct place to touch a woman's hand during courtship. A mere touch on the hand was considered erotic enough to cause a woman to feel giddy with delight. The nineteenth century was the Age of Romanticism in which chastity was highly valued, and love was spiritually idealized. This behavior may have been sufficient for the romantic fantasies of couples during Victorian times, but twentieth century men and women felt no nostalgia for the saccharine sweetness of romantic relationships of past generations. Both men and women clamored for change.

TODAY

The twentieth century was ushered in with the philosophy of Sigmund Freud exhorting us to liberate our *Id* and follow its demand to obtain immediate pleasure in our lives. Freud's philosophy also stated that sex is a prime motivator in a person's life. It followed that there was little time for romance in a relationship unless it resulted in sexual gratification. This influence, combined with the emergence of the first-wave feminist movement, expanded a woman's awareness of their own physical needs. She knew what she wanted and didn't want to waste any time getting it.

The silent film star Rudolph Valentino defined a new aspect of romance. Women were eager to give up their romantic fantasies of a handholding, poetry-reading lover like Heathcliff and Byron in exchange for a tango dancing, brooding, perfumed silk pajama-wearing, sexy seducer of women.

Although some blamed Valentino for feminizing the American male; men called *Vaselinos* copied his persona by slicking back their hair with Vaseline, dressing glamorously, and brushing up on their dancing skills. Animal magnetism replaced all other forms of romantic attraction. Valentino was a bit of a misogynist who probably would have been comfortable hanging out with our fictional Buddy. His bold proclamation that women "like to have a masterful man" might be construed by some to be a chauvinistic remark. Nonetheless, the flappers and other women in the 1920s idolized Valentino.

EVEN THOUGH SEX appeal was now considered an important part of the equation, romance persevered. In 1936, Edward VIII married American divorcée Wallis Simpson and abdicated the throne as king of the United Kingdom, and the world felt all warm and fuzzy over a real-life Cinderella story. Although not everyone could recreate this amorous scenario of life in a palace, the happy ending of the love affair of Simpson and Edward VIII helped erase the stigma of a divorced woman being stale goods and acknowledged the equality of two partners in a relationship.

Despite the glamour and publicity surrounding the romantic pursuits of famous couples in the 1930s and 1940s, the average man and woman were content to more quietly pursue romance. As a teenager, I can recall being embarrassed at my parent's New Year's Eve party when my father grabbed my mother and pulled her to a spot under a piece of mistletoe. He then took her in his arms, tipped her over, and gave her a kiss worthy of any Tinseltown film. Although there was no media present to record this moment, I always thought that it was pretty romantic. From the loud cheering, it would seem that the partygoers agreed with me.

Women in the 1950s slow danced, went steady, and were pinned. The goal was still to get a *Mrs.* degree, but women could have fun and push the limits a bit while pursuing this goal if they observed certain rules of behavior. The man was still the dominant partner in a relationship, deciding when to pursue a woman. He could be polite, open doors, bestow corsages, and use his manliness to attract a mate. Women read "How to Get a Husband" manuals that blessed petting and necking if it was done with the person they planned to marry. Romance was great, but finding a lifelong mate was the most important goal in a woman's life.

—

THE WORLD EXPLODED in the 1960s and 1970s when women asserted their equality in all things, including sexual behavior. The National Organization for Women (NOW) was founded and promoted women's rights. Women dressed as they pleased, had control over childbearing, held important jobs, initiated dating, and they wouldn't hesitate to file for divorce if things turned sour. Love was no longer tied to romance. Free love and hooking up became the buzzwords of the day. A woman didn't need to be wooed. If she liked what she saw, she just took it. Men benefited from women's new attitude regarding romance in relationships as now they were no longer under pressure to keep the spark of romance alive.

Some couple's passions for each other were so volatile that their ensuing romance took on epic proportions. On March 15, 1964, two of the most famous movie stars of the time, Elizabeth Taylor and Richard Burton, married. They had fallen in love on the set of the movie *Cleopatra* where fittingly Taylor played Cleopatra and Burton played her lover, Marc Anthony. In an instant, their film romance transformed into an intense and dramatic real-life love affair. It was indeed an affair because both Taylor and Burton were married at the time. Although their union was labeled the marriage of the century, it caused such a scandal that even the Pope publicly commented it. From the beginning of their affair, it was clear that their romance was based on lust, an over-the-top extravagant lifestyle, and the thrill of the chase. Instead of gifts of roses and candy, Burton gave Taylor the first million-dollar diamond ever sold, and on her thirty-second birthday; he surprised her with Casa Kimberly, a nine-bedroom villa in Puerto Vallarta. Their tumultuous romance wasn't all sweet mutterings and soft caresses. The couple would engage in violent fights in public, especially when Taylor was high on pills, and Burton was drunk. Occasionally, as Burton would say, they would fight "purely for the exercise."

Throughout their marriage, both parties cheated and eventually divorced in 1974. However, their all-consuming love for each other led them to remarry a year after this first divorce in 1975, only to ultimately divorce again for good in 1976. In 1973, Taylor said about her relationship with Burton, "When you are in love and lust like that, you just grab it with both hands and ride out the storm." Perhaps the excitement of their relationship's storminess is what fueled their romance. Undeniably, an important component of Burton and Taylor's romance was the continual rides that they took together on the roller coaster of drama and lust. Taylor says it best in her letter to Burton on their tenth anniversary, "I lust thee."

ALTHOUGH THE STATUS of women vastly improved during the 1970s, many inequities still existed between men and women, as evidenced by the disparity of pay and the continued rejection of the Equal Rights Amendment (ERA). Nonetheless, women had gained a spot on the playing field, so once again, they could focus on romance in their relationships.

In the 1980s, instead of men sending women poetry, it became popular for men to send to a potential girlfriend something called mixtapes, a compilation of music expressing romantic sentiments. These weren't commercial recordings, rather they were made by individuals who would select specific songs that conveyed a message of love.

By the end of the twentieth century, the fast pace of modern life made creating song lists and writing love letters passé as tools for courting. The emergence of the internet into everyday people's homes made it possible for couples to more expeditiously get to know one another. In addition, engaging in physical intimacy became risky because of the sexually transmitted disease HIV/AIDS. Mortality rates related to the disease peaked in 1995. Many people soon questioned if a romantic relationship was worth dying for.

This lack of physicality led to the popularity of online dating on sites like Match.com, which was launched in 1995. Emails and emoticons replaced love letters. It was effortless but left a lot to be desired if a woman was hoping to be seduced by her man at a candlelight dinner with champagne and roses. This endless search for romance was depicted in the show *Sex and the City*, which debuted in 1998. Carrie, Samantha, Miranda, and Charlotte epitomized the emancipated career woman who was finally able to enjoy sex like a man. Nonetheless, our four women still remained wistful about the lack of that certain something in their relationships. Did this equality of a woman's and man's sexuality make romance no longer viable?

Each generation has its own interpretation of what constitutes romance. Relationships are spiced up because of many variables. The average person may experience some dramatic events in their relationship, but we usually don't share them, at least not publicly. Instead, we live vicariously through famous couples such as Angelina Jolie and Brad Pitt. Pitt had cheated on his wife, Jennifer Aniston, when he decided he couldn't resist Jolie. Did the subsequent scandal add some zest to Pitt and Aniston's relationship?

Megan Markle and Prince Harry showed the world that it was worth giving up a kingdom for their great romance. Perhaps Will Smith believed he was being gallant when at the Academy Awards show he slapped Chris Rock to defend the honor of his wife. Was it romance that caused Angelina, Brad, Megan, Harry, and Will to take these actions? Or is it just that fame makes some people do strange things?

—

BECAUSE OF THE many variables in society affecting women's and men's roles, it's no surprise that the concept of romance is so misunderstood. This confusion might have a bearing on the belief that romance is dead in the twenty-first century. Millennials and Gen Z have sex less frequently, and when they do date it is often impersonal and through online platforms like Tinder and Bumble. Texting is the latest way to talk as it's quick and to the point, as is sex, which often occurs on the first date without any bells and whistles. There is no rush to get married as noted by statista.com. They state that as of 2020, only 44 percent of millennials aged twenty-three to thirty-eight were married.

Women no longer hope to emulate the romantically tremulous relationship between Jane Eyre and Mr. Rochester in the book *Jane Eyre*, or the loyal devotion between lovers exemplified in *The Notebook*. Their newly found empowerment now attracts them to films like *Mr.*

& Mrs. Smith and *Kill Bill,* films that portray women as badass assassins who trade in the traditional attributes of romance in exchange for the nuanced excitement of hand-to-hand combat with a sexy opponent.

Romance may not be dead, but it has dramatically changed from the biblical age to the present day. With that in mind, let's find out how our respondents of both surveys answered the question, How do you define romance? Men's responses by percentage are as follows.

MEN'S RESPONSES

RESPONSES	PERCENTAGE
No idea/doesn't exist	27
Love	27
Sex	16
Affection	12
Emotions/hormones	11
Respect/trust	4
Gifts/flowers etc.	3

As you can see, we have a tie between two disparate categories. The male respondents either said that they didn't have a clue about the meaning of romance because it probably doesn't exist, or that romance and love are one and the same. I still wonder about the middling number of responses declaring that romance is sex. Hopefully, these low numbers don't reflect the fact that men were afraid to answer candidly, despite the anonymity of the survey. The three categories with the highest percentages line up with twentieth century research indicating that men today either don't know how to be romantic or they think that once they proclaim their love for a woman that they've completed their job in the romance department. On the other hand, some of the men's comments below show a touching sentimentality that indicates there may be a few romanticists hiding behind stoic, manly personas.

- "Smile, flowers, laughter, tears, chocolate."
- "Two hearts beating as one."
- "I've been there, and it can't be beat."
- "A beneficial loss of reality."
- "Being stung by Cupid's arrow."

But then, unfortunately, some answers like the following three make you feel sorry for any woman involved with a man who thinks in such a calculating, passionless way.

- "A false construct created by advertisers to sell more products."
- "Persuading someone for sex."
- "Doing things for your woman to make her happy and get what you want from her."

"No idea/doesn't exist" was the only category in which the women's answers came close to what the men answered. Also, women ranked "Sex" with the same percentage as "No idea/doesn't exist," while men scored it third in importance.

WOMEN'S RESPONSES

RESPONSES	PERCENTAGE
No idea/doesn't exist	26
Sex	26
Gifts/Flowers etc.	24
Love	9
Affection	7
Respect/trust	5
Emotions/hormones	3

As indicated, women rated gifts as a highly important component of romance. A hint to any man reading this: It might be wise to dig into your wallet if you want the woman in your life to feel special. The following sampling of women's comments shows that many women are jaded about a man's romantic intentions.

- "There is no romance, only delusional fantasies on their part (men) where women are nothing more than a figment of their imagination."
- "Just enough to get her to sleep with him."
- "A few drinks then sex."
- "McDonald's and a movie."
- "They'd ask what it is."

Let's be honest, there's no magical formula guaranteeing that a man and woman with a humdrum love life will blossom into a modern-day Romeo and Juliet. Many women would prefer Noah's and Jim's approach to romance to that of Buddy's. However, these women might have a difficult time finding their very own Lord Bryon because the responses to our men's survey shows that a significant number of men think that sex is the ultimate romantic gesture. At the very least, a person's innate drive to find a mate will lead them to search for ways to fulfill their partner's romantic fantasies, even if they have to fake their own inclinations. There's no denying that some form of attraction is needed for romance to develop. It's evident that men are enticed by a woman's sexuality, so next we need to look at what attributes men think make women sexy.

CHAPTER 4

THE FEMALE ATTRIBUTES THAT DRIVE MEN WILD

You can almost guarantee that there will be some chuckles or ribald comments anytime the word *sex* is part of a conversation between men, as you will see in this month's conversation between Jim, Buddy, and Noah.

The three men decide to finish their first drink before they tackle the subject that has occupied their minds since they went through puberty. But it has only been talked about jokingly between them. Buddy can be heard muttering under his breath, "Sex, it's finally a subject that I can teach these guys a thing or two about." But the real question is what attributes does a man think makes a woman sexy?

Jim rushes to be the first one to speak as he just wants to get his part of the discussion finished. He explains to his friends that he thinks that a woman's sex appeal depends on many variables. He says, "To be honest, the attributes that I find sexy in my wife are very different from those qualities that attracted me to a girl when I was a teenager. As a young boy, I was infatuated with the image of a sexpot with exaggerated breasts and buttocks that were featured in men's magazines. These women were the stars in many of my dreams. Occasionally, I got lucky and went out on a date with a well-endowed woman, but it wasn't too long before I felt that something was missing in the chemistry between us. And then, I met the woman who would become my future wife. She had a nice figure and was more than I could hope for in the looks department, but what fascinated me most was her personality."

He continues. "Although many of the women whom I had dated in the past were experts in flirtation, I was intrigued by the challenges my future wife, Claire, brought to our interactions. Claire was strongly opinionated and didn't believe in playing games to attract a man. She knew what she wanted and didn't hesitate to show her physical passion for me. This passion also extended to her love for engaging with me in spirited debates about world events. She quickly lost patience with conversations about the latest fashions or television shows. Although Claire might seem to have an alpha female personality, she made it clear that she also wanted to someday be a wife and mother. I can't imagine a more scintillating combination of characteristics to define *sexiness* in a woman than intelligence, sensuality, and a nurturing disposition. I found Claire's self-confidence a real turn on." Jim suspected that Buddy might not agree with his sentiments regarding a woman's sexiness, because in the past Buddy's comments about women indicated that a woman's less cerebral qualities excited Buddy.

Jim glances at Buddy to gauge his friend's reaction. Now, it was Buddy's turn to speak. "If a woman's figure measures 38-26-41 like Kim Kardashian, then I don't care if she's a Rhodes scholar or barely able to read. The mere thought of myself with such a goddess is enough to get me excited. I don't care if we don't exchange a word."

Buddy catches Jim and Noah exchanging glances, so he decides to back up his perspective on a woman's sexiness by referring to some internet research he had done about sexual attraction. He tells his friends, "Scientific studies show that sexual chemistry is based on the attraction to someone's physical attributes. These physical attributes cause our brains to release high levels of testosterone, estrogen, dopamine, and norepinephrine. These hormones and pleasure chemicals incite us to seek sexual gratification, and for me, that gratification depends on the desirability of a woman's body." Buddy then proudly declares to his friends that there is even research that was published in the *Archives of Sexual Behavior* that underscore the validity of his viewpoint. He tells them that he's not alone in his seemingly caveman attitude toward sexual attraction. "The study revealed that men generally looked most at the chest and waist-hip ratio when evaluating a woman for a potential relationship."

Now that Buddy showed his friends that he was more than an ignorant dolt he continued to explain his feelings. "Jim, I'm not sure that I understand what you just said about what female attributes you find attractive." Buddy continued, "It sounds like you were saying that you got turned on by a woman who constantly tested you. I can't believe that you could think that confrontation is sexy. It also seems strange to me that you'd enjoy a woman taking the lead in the lovemaking department. When I think of a sexy woman, I imagine someone who looks at me to take the lead in the relationship. I don't like being questioned or having to prove my point to someone. A challenge to me is seeing how long it takes to get a woman into bed, not mentally sparring with her. In my mind, a sexy woman will of course, have a great body. But more importantly, she has to know how to use it. She needs to have a soft voice and understand that I'll have the final word in all things. I'm not looking for a woman who possesses masculine traits. I have male friends for that. In a nutshell, a sexy woman needs to know her place in the world, and that place is subservient to her man." Buddy believes that he is the only one of the trio who is being honest, and if either of his friends is startled by his candor, then they need to look deep into their hearts to explore whether they feel the same way.

Noah thanks Jim and Buddy for sharing and admits that his feelings are a combination of both Jim's and Buddy's perspectives. Noah explains. "When I first met Jane, I couldn't take my eyes off her. She exuded sexuality with her short skirts, breathy way of speaking, and flirtatious manner. In addition, my ego was constantly stroked by Jane's deference to me as our teacher-student scenario enhanced my sense of control in the dynamics of our relationship. What man wouldn't enjoy strutting around with eye candy on his arm? However, it wasn't too long before I realized that something distinguished Jane from the many other stunning women who crossed my path. The sexiness that oozed out of Jane was simply a part of who she was, not something fabricated to lure me to her."

Noah continued. "As I got to know Jane better, it became clear to me that what I thought was deference to my masculinity was actually Jane's focused determination to elicit from me any pearls of wisdom that she could incorporate into her knowledge base. It was almost like Jane was a vampire who got stronger as she drank a person's blood, and Jane did get stronger. By the time we were officially a couple, Jane was totally secure in her goals in life. I was no longer her mentor, as she could now not only hold her own in conversations with me but frequently had me searching Google to buttress my opinions. I guess you could say that Jane was the total package. No one would ever compare her to an empty box disguised by sensational gift wrap. At the end of the day, the bottom half of my body appreciated Jane's obvious physical allure, but my heart and brain were addicted to her intelligence and vivaciousness."

Jim, Buddy, and Noah obviously have different ideas about the attributes that make a woman sexy. Let's find out how their feelings match up with the ideas of men of past generations.

YESTERDAY

Although it's generally accepted that the sexual revolution began in the 1960s, the people of Minoan Greece back in the year 3,600 BC were no prudes when it came to expressing their sexuality. Women weren't afraid to play up their best features to attract a mate. Frescoes of Minoan women indicate that their appearance was sensual. Kiss curls on their foreheads, red lips, and revealing clothing all point to a type of sexual liberation. Depictions of these women rarely show them as mothers but instead have them fighting bulls and being served by others. The perfect hourglass figure was the height of fashion for women during these times. Women were shown with bare breasts and corseted, pinched waists. Minoan males were conditioned by the society that they lived in to desire women who were independent, sexually liberated, and powerful. It's doubtful if these men would get turned on by the image of a virginal, submissive female.

The pendulum regarding sexuality swung radically between the free expression of the Minoans to the biblical era's emphasis on female spiritual attractiveness. The Bible describes Sarah as "a woman of beautiful countenance" (Genesis 12:11). Although Sarah was ninety, Abraham was still worried about losing her to the Pharoah when they traveled to Egypt. Apparently, youth and an unblemished face didn't carry that much weight in a man's sexual attraction to a woman during the time of Abraham. A woman was sought after if she exuded beauty from within and possessed traits that made her a good wife and mother.

On the other hand, not all men during these times worshipped virtuous women. The biblical book of the Song of Songs, found among the *Dead Sea Scrolls*, celebrates pleasure for pleasure's sake. Images created by the poem's words, "he shall lie all night betwixt my breasts," tell us that probably a lot more was going on than praying during these holy times. Stories abound of alluring women like Delilah, who uses her sexuality to strip Samson of his power. By all accounts, it was her voluptuousness, not saintliness, that made Samson succumb to her seduction.

Jumping ahead to ancient and classical Greece and Rome, differing criteria was used to define female sensuality depending on a woman's role in society.

Ancient Greek women looked up to the goddess Aphrodite with her round face, large breasts, and pear-shaped body, and redheads were considered the epitome of beauty. However, female physical appearance hardly seemed important to men when considering marriage. The paramount quality for women to possess was the ability to bear children and care for their families. This didn't mean that Greek men were blind to a woman's sexual charms. The culture of the day addressed men's sexual needs by classifying sexual pleasure as the type of love involved in the relationship. *Agape* and *storge* were the names for the love of a spouse or family member, while *eros* was an entirely different type of love. It was a passionate, erotic love, and generally a man didn't engage in this type of love with his wife. Greek men hired Hetaira women for sexual and intellectual fulfillment. Hetaira women were well-educated and versed in conversation, dance, and music, but more importantly, they were beautiful and eager to sexually satisfy the man who paid for their companionship. It was believed that sex should never be a thing of pleasure for a Greek wife. Instead, she must appear chaste at all times while her husband was free to indulge his sexual appetite at drinking parties called *symposia*.

Although female Greek goddesses were admired for their beauty, the most eminent adoration was reserved for the male body. The splendor of the male body is evidenced in Greek art in which fully clothed women are depicted next to nude males. Homosexuality wasn't just accepted; it was considered the purest form of love. Based on what I've read about Greek history, the attribute that made a Greek woman sexy was her willingness to satisfy a man sexually. The Hetaira were praised for this skill.

Much of the Roman attitude toward female sexuality was inherited from the ancient Greeks. There was only one glaring difference in what Greek and Roman men found sexy— the size of a woman's breasts. Greek men wanted their women to have large breasts while Roman men found small breasts sexy. In ancient Rome, breasts were associated with a mother's role of nursing infants, and this image was anathema to Roman men when it came to sexual attraction. Large breasts were so ridiculed that young girls wore a tight-fitting type of strapless bra to restrain their breasts. Imagine the horror in a Roman man's eyes if a modern-day Beyoncé suddenly appeared in their midst. Beyoncé does have a saving grace to counter her well-endowed chest. She has abundant hips, and this was something that was greatly prized in ancient Rome, as it was considered a good indication of a woman's fertility.

Respectable women were supposed to express their sexual

passions only in marriage and were taught to emulate female purity as epitomized by the Vestal virgins who were required to remain chaste for thirty years. On the other hand, Roman men were raised to be physically dominant, and it was natural and acceptable for them to engage in sexual relations with youths of both sexes. Perhaps the most important characteristic required of a sexual partner in ancient Roman times was that they be submissive. However, even these criteria weren't set in stone, as evidenced by the wild passion that Caesar had for Cleopatra, who, as we all know, was anything but submissive. It's pretty evident that there were some odd perceptions of what made a woman sexually attractive throughout the centuries.

In Medieval Japan, women dyed their teeth black and totally plucked off their eyebrows to then repaint them close to their hairline. The size of a woman's breast didn't matter as her body was hidden under a robe comprised of between ten-to-forty layers of silk.

During the Renaissance, there were rigid criteria for women. The sexy Renaissance woman had a receding hairline, pale skin, fine blond hair, and was definitely plump. A double chin was a bonus. Some of the beauty standards resulted in injury or even death. To achieve the sought after pale skin a woman used a whitening product called Venetian ceruse. This product's main ingredient was lead. For many women, this meant that the price of beauty was the risk of being poisoned. Some women were lucky and only lost all their hair because they were using sulfuric acid to dye it that perfect blond.

THE NINETEENTH CENTURY again saw a resurgence of the desirability of the hourglass figure, although this flaunting of the female figure seemed contradictory to the puritanical attitude that still existed toward a woman's sexuality. One of the few places where a woman could flaunt her voluptuous figure was as a performer in film or on the stage.

The actress Lillian Russell had a full, statuesque figure. She was considered the nineteenth century ideal of American female beauty and sexuality. She was so alluring to men that one of her boyfriends gave her a gold-plated, diamond-inlaid bicycle made by Tiffany's. But Russell was the exception to the rule governing sex appeal in a woman during Victorian times. A woman's clothing was supposed to signify that her domain was her home, not riding a bicycle or strutting around on a stage. Tight corsets and long skirts signaled that she did not participate in vigorous activities. It was an age of repression in which even sex during marriage was condemned by the prudish. Women were advised in relationship guides that a good way to avoid their husbands' overly amorous advances was to excuse themselves to go to the toilet.

Cleanliness attracted a man to a woman. It was believed that cleanliness equaled godliness and respectability, and these virtues were supposedly more arousing to a man than a hug or a kiss. A woman's overt sexuality had less appeal than a clean kitchen sink in Victorian times. However, prostitution and pornography were rampant because it was an accepted fact that men shouldn't repress their sexual desires. Apparently, they just shouldn't satisfy these desires with their wives.

TODAY

By the beginning of the twentieth century the emergence of the flapper demonstrated an abrupt change in both women's clothing and roles, which exerted a tremendous influence on what was considered a woman's sexual attractiveness. Full figures and corsets went out the window. A flapper was extremely lean with a boyish figure, cropped hair, short dresses, and a painted face. Men responded favorably to this new look as it indicated a freedom and engagement with life that they found exciting.

But this *joie de vie* didn't last throughout all of the twentieth century. Unfortunately, it wasn't until the 1960s that the wild cry of the flapper for freedom was again heard. The years following World

War II presented confusion among gender roles. Women took over men's jobs while the men fought, and in some cases many women even served in the military. Unfortunately, instead of society focusing on the contributions of these women, magazines were advising women in uniform, "Remember that your duty as a woman, uniform or no uniform, is to be feminine come what may" (Woman, January 1940). During the war Victory girls and Good Girls existed to provide *comfort* to servicemen. In the past, these types of services would be considered prostitution and yet were now accepted as a necessity of war. Many men of this time also believed that their masculinity was threatened by women assuming traditionally male roles, such as working in factories or serving in the military.

There was an attempt in the years following the war to return to a world where men were the protective leaders, and sex was controlled. In the 1940s, *Esquire* magazine created a quiz that had men answer specific questions about what they thought was attractive in a woman. Their answers demonstrate that they wanted a demure, yet sensual looking woman. They didn't like women who drank too much because they believed it was a sign that these women were promiscuous. They also didn't like women wearing sensible clothing, and they took pride in their wife or girlfriend getting admiring glances because of her glamorous clothing. The men didn't want their women hanging out with unattractive friends because the men enjoyed having more pretty women to look at. They thought it was sexy when their woman complimented them. But horror of all horrors, men abhorred a woman doing things with her hands while she was talking to them. In their minds, hand movement was a tease because it implied a woman was offering sexual favors. This is so crazy that it made me believe that men who believed such nonsense must have been mentally damaged during the war.

These ridiculous gender biases led to the 1950s' rigid guidelines for a woman's role in society. Women were now back in the home. Their successful forays into doing things that were in the past considered men's work were quickly forgotten. High heels, clinched waistlines in dresses, sexy undergarments, a practical apron, and white gloves were all essential clothing for the '50s women, and yes, although hard to believe, the hourglass figure was once again back. Women were confused by the schizophrenic definition of their role in society. Sex symbols like Brigitte Bardot and Marilyn Monroe were the personification of the sexually emancipated woman with a hedonistic lifestyle. Monroe proved that her sex appeal could even get her a relationship with the president of the United States. Men, apparently even JFK, wanted their women looking like Monroe and Bardot but these women also needed to look like a lady to assume their primary responsibility in society of caring for the family and home.

TWIGGY WAS THE new sex symbol of the 1960s and 70s, and as her name implied, she was rail thin with a flat chest and buttocks. This look became the new standard for men to judge a female's sexual attractiveness. Strangely enough, its androgynous fashion helped women break from the exaggerated feminism of the past decades. Youth was also lauded as a woman's lack of curves highlighted her childlike look. These characteristics were a striking departure from the qualities that attracted men in the past to women.

The late twentieth century was a time of great growth in women's status in the world. Women now were CEOs of major companies, had a say in childbearing, and expressed their sexual needs without fear of retribution. They wore what they liked, and their hair was long, short, or in between. Individuality was the keyword. Social media was not as intrusive as it is today, so women could do their own thing.

Smart was in. Even Revlon at the time proclaimed that *Smart is Sexxxy*. Men agreed. Supermodels like Cindy Crawford and Claudia Schiff became the new sex symbols of the 1990s. They were stylish and polished looking women whose ethereal beauty made them just a little out of reach of the average male. In addition, women like Heidi Klum showed the world that she could be the star of every man's fantasy and still hold her own with male power brokers. She began her career as one of the most recognizable Victoria's Secret angels. After working thirteen years as an angel, she used her fame to partner with Victoria's Secret to launch a lingerie and cosmetics line, and without ever setting foot into an elite business school, she was on her way toward becoming a multi-millionaire. Her brand included numerous items of clothing for men and women, shoes, jewelry, and perfume. She started a successful acting career and from there, she went on to host and produce shows such as Project Runway. She personified the woman who could do and have everything. She's the loving mother to her three children whom she had with her ex-husband, the singer, Sting. On the other hand, she is a sexy siren who was able to attract and marry her second husband who is sixteen years her junior, while simultaneously achieving her goals as a savvy businesswoman. As of 2023, her net worth, according to Celebrity Net Worth, is $160 million. She can bring home the bacon, cook it, and feed it to her man in bed. What man could resist those attributes?

The most outstanding example of the exploitation of a woman's sexuality in the twentieth century can be observed in the success of *Playboy* magazine. The first issue was published in 1953 featuring Marilyn Monroe as Playmate of the Month. Many men can remember hiding it under their mattresses and surreptitiously opening up the centerfold to fantasize about that month's Playmate. The magazine is a treasure trove of statistics describing the "perfect" female for each decade. In the 1950s, 1960s, and 1970s, these criteria never varied much. A Playmate had blond hair, was between eighteen and twenty-three, was about 5'4" tall, weighed about 115 pounds, and most importantly had very full breasts. Of course, she also had to be willing to pose nude. This hourglass figure became more toned, thin hipped and athletic looking in the 1980s. In the 1990s, Playmate became a brand of its own. Playmates became celebrities and didn't hesitate to enhance their looks with plastic surgery. It's believed that Hugh Hefner spent seventy thousand dollars a year on breast implants for his Playmates. Nonetheless, Hefner believed that even these beautiful women could use more help than even surgical enhancements could provide. Playboy photographer Josh Ryan used his magical airbrushing techniques to put the finishing touches to these women's photos. These touch ups included giving a tuck and trim to a female's pelvic area, removing blemishes and tattoos, and enlarging or reducing breasts. The average woman couldn't compete with these examples of unflawed female sexuality. Playboy's ultimate goal was to make the Playmates incite desire and fantasy for the male reader. The phenomenal sale numbers of this magazine left no question as to what female attributes men thought were sexy during these decades.

Hefner built on the success of his magazine by opening Playboy Clubs, in which a playboy could further entertain his fantasies when being served food and drink by a Playboy Bunny. Hefner believed that an actual animal bunny symbolized sexuality because it was shy, yet sexy. He modeled his human female bunnies on this concept. The Bunnies working in his clubs had hourglass figures and wore waist-clinching, breast-enhancing bunny outfits that included a fluffy cottontail. However, it was understood that they had to maintain a persona of the well-washed girl next door rather than a *femme fatale*. There were rigid guidelines that had to be followed, including no drinking alcoholic beverages or chewing gum. They had to wear vivid lipstick, maintain their cottontails in pristine condition, and refrigerate their hosiery after use. The only jewelry they could wear was Playboy cufflinks. Any transgressions could result in dismissal. This alluring Bunny could be looked at but not touched. Controversy existed over whether these human bunnies perpetuated the objectification of women. Even the name, *Playmate* suggested a male-female relationship in which the female is a toy to be used for a man's enjoyment. Apparently, men eventually became uncomfortable with the message associated with the Playboy brand. The only clubs still existing today are pop-up ones at events like Art Basel in Miami, and *Playboy* magazine is now only published digitally online.

THE TWENTY-FIRST CENTURY entertained a peculiar dichotomy concerning acknowledgment of female attractiveness. It was acknowledged that women enjoyed being appreciated for their sensuality, and yet a societal taboo existed that censured men who valued a woman's physical attributes. Women believed that they had the same rights as men in all aspects of life, including their sexual relationships, and yet men who helped them exercise these rights were condemned. During this time, the MeToo movement was gaining in notoriety. Men and women were having a difficult time balancing their longings with socially acceptable passions. Walls began to go up, until social dating platforms came along. These new platforms evened the playing field as all genders could pick their new partners with the click of a key. This also meant that men and women could filter their matchups by designating desired characteristics in potential male suitors.

The reality, however, is that the most physically attractive people got the most clicks. Men were inspired by the Hollywood beauty exemplified in famous women of the day such as Scarlett Johansson, Angelina Jolie, Beyoncé, and Jennifer Lopez. These women definitely didn't have big bellies, or shaved eyebrows, or the receding hairlines that were prized female characteristics in past decades. These women were classic beauties with toned bodies, perfectly proportioned faces, and glistening hair. They had achieved the pinnacle of success in their fields. The twenty-first century woman was the total package of looks, sensuality, and brains. Unfortunately, a man might be disappointed if he was searching an online dating platform for a woman with the attributes of an Angelina or Jennifer. A man might not swipe right (that means he likes her) on a woman who could have other qualities that enhance her sensuality. Just like women, men in the twenty-first century have been taught that they too can have it all.

MEN LIKE OUR friend Buddy didn't have to worry if their concept of what defines a "sexy" woman is offensive to some women because these men needn't mention their proclivities online. It's forbidden for a man to say that he finds an overweight woman with a face that definitely wouldn't launch a thousand ships sexually unattractive, but with online platforms, no one needs to know his real thoughts as he can let his fingers do the talking without censure. Although today's women may have a seat in the boardroom or on the basketball court, it seems that there is still pressure for them to look a certain way to attract a man on a dating platform if she wants to get that important click.

Our survey respondents didn't have to worry about being called out for offending any woman with their answers to the question, "What attributes do you think make a woman sexy?" as the anonymity of the survey gave them the freedom to express their true feelings. Here are the men's responses by percentage showing what attributes they thought made a woman sexy.

MEN'S RESPONSES

ATTRIBUTE	PERCENTAGE
Appearance of Face/Shape	38
Intellect	17
Character/Confidence	15
Don't know	15
Personality	9
Sense of humor	4
Concern for the man	2

Some of the men's comments are lewd, so I've excluded them from this chapter. I think that you might already have some idea about the content of these responses that focus on a woman's body parts, so let's look at some of the more introspective comments.

- "Eyes, you can see if she's telling you the truth or not."
- "They have their life together."
- "Up to the eye of the beholder. It's subjective."
- "Sexy is more of a pejorative term than a term of endearment. A woman is generally sexy because she wants to be. She dresses in a more risqué manner, wears excessive makeup, and conducts herself in a manner to attract someone to mate with (or just to get a free meal)."

Our last respondent seems a little jaded about what constitutes sexiness in a woman, but at least he's not hung up on focusing solely on a woman's body parts. Our survey indicates that a woman can have a lousy personality, no sense of humor, and not give a damn about the man she's trying to attract, yet she can still be sexy in a man's eyes. However, it's encouraging to note that quite a few men appreciate intelligence and character in a woman. Both men and women survey respondents ranked appearance in the first-place position, but the percentage of women's responses attributing body and face with sexual attractiveness is almost double that of the men's responses. None of the women indicated that concern for the man contributed to making a woman sexy. It seems that they just didn't give a damn. The women's responses are:

WOMEN'S RESPONSES

ATTRIBUTE	PERCENTAGE
Appearance of Face/Shape	64
Character/Confidence	12

Intellect	10
Sense of humor	6
Personality	4
Don't know	4
Concern for the man	0

Most of our female respondent's comments regarding sex appeal emphasize the importance of a woman's body and her submissiveness to the man.

- "Good figure and a dirty mind."
- "Sexy clothes that show cleavage, makeup, a good figure with a narrow waist and ample bosom, listening to the man and being concerned about his comfort, keeping her mouth shut, no interrupting or disputing what he says."
- "Beautiful face, curvaceous figure and submissive attitude."
- "A message put out that they are easy to have sex with, either implied or spoken directly."

The women portrayed in the TV miniseries, *The Handmaid's Tale*, would almost fulfill these qualifications for sexy if only they'd throw away their hoods and cloaks.

Although intelligence was not a decisive factor in the men's comments regarding a woman's sexiness, it's important to find out if smart women actually turn men on or off. You'll find out in the next chapter.

CHAPTER 5

SMARTY PANTS OR HOT PANTS: WHAT TURNS A MAN ON?

The surveys' answers to the question, "What attributes make a woman sexy?" It make it clear that intelligence was not at the top of the list for sex appeal. However, we still need to find out if men are actually turned off by brainy women, such as those depicted in movies like *The Devil Wears Prada*. In this movie the female boss is an unapproachable ice goddess who is demanding and is smarter than anyone working for her. She personifies many of the character traits of a traditional male leader and prioritizes her job over family and friends, resulting in multiple divorces. Her interactions with men appear asexual. Is it possible that this movie's sensibilities were elicited from real-life scenarios?

Society has traditionally accepted the notion that women should defer to men's superior intellect. Flipping this belief could be perceived as a threat to the balance of power in male-female relationships. Does a man possess sufficient self-esteem in order to not only acknowledge intelligence in a woman but to actually find it a stimulating turn on? Why don't we see what our three men in the bar can tell us about this.

The world of finance has recently opened its doors to women with them holding more than half of the entry-level finance jobs. However, fewer than one in ten of the top public financial institutions have women in senior positions. Jim's firm deserves congratulations as it has numerous women in senior roles. When Jim finds himself in competition with one of these women he reacts as he would with one of his male coworkers. He wants to beat them in whatever task he's performing. But there is something that Jim rarely admits about his interactions with these female executives. He can barely acknowledge to himself that the reason that he finds it exciting to demonstrate his intelligence to a smart woman is that he views this kind of communication as a harmless form of flirtation. He believes that this type of synergy is rare within lower ranking female coworkers because he's not competing with them. Jim tells his friends, "Although my wife Claire doesn't possess financial acumen like the women executives in my firm, she more than matches or surpasses me in mental acuity relating to most other things in life. I don't understand the appeal of an uninformed woman. I could get a pet if all I want is affection. I'm captivated by the back-and-forth dialogue with someone who challenges me, but to be honest, it's even more exciting if our discourse ends with Claire complimenting me for my knowledge." Jim's condescending assumption that a person's job level is a determinant of their intelligence might anger many men and women. Implying that he possesses superior brainpower adds to his arrogance.

BUDDY IS SHAKING his head in disbelief as he glares dismissively at Jim and Noah. "You guys are real wimps," says Buddy. "For the past several months we've sat together at this bar, and I've listened to you talk about women as if you're reading from a textbook listing men's socially acceptable sentiment about them. I think that I'm the only guy here who is expressing his real thoughts. When it comes to whether smart women turn me on, I can unequivocally say *no, never*, not in this lifetime."

Buddy is flushed just thinking about dating a smart woman and continues his tirade. "I want a woman to look up to me and to realize that I'm the dominant one in the relationship. My word shouldn't be questioned whether, ultimately, I'm right or wrong." Jim and Noah don't know whether Buddy is joking or a time traveler from the 1950s. Buddy says, "When I meet a smart woman, a certain part of my body deflates." Noah interrupts Buddy. "Hey guys, I've got to cut it short tonight as I need to get some sleep so I can catch an early flight to New York tomorrow morning, but I want to contribute to this discussion." He continues. "I have to strongly object to Buddy alluding that Jim's and my opinions about women make us wimps. It takes a secure, confident man to appreciate the allure of a smart woman. I think that Buddy is afraid that he won't be able to hold his own in a matchup with a smart woman, and that she will belittle him. Now that I've said my piece, I need to get out of here before our lively discussion turns into an argument that none of us want to have."

Noah's comments have acknowledged the elephant in the room. Does a man's attraction to a smart woman actually depend on a woman's behavior, or is this attraction determined on whether the man is secure in who he is?

Now that our three guys have given us some idea of whether smart women are a turn on or turn off for them, we need to look at different periods in history to discover if during these times men considered smart women desirable.

YESTERDAY

The historical authenticity of stories from the Bible is often taken with a grain of salt, but in 1993 in Northern Israel, archaeologists discovered fragments of a monument dated around 835 BC that mentioned the defeat of Israel by the king of Damascus. It also alluded to the House of David. This fact makes the Bible's reference to King David and Abigail more compelling, as it is a recounting of something that actually happened.

Abigail was the wife of Nabal. He was a despicable character lacking common sense. Nabal insulted David by refusing to give him a small amount of food supplies, and now David was on his way to Nabal's home with four hundred men to extract his revenge. Abigail was an intelligent woman who realized that it was up to her to use her brains to remove her household from danger. She went to David with supplies, prostrated herself on the ground before him, and explained that her husband was a man of bad character, but that God would not want David to kill him just because of his foolishness. Because of Abigail's words, David realized that he had let his anger get the best of him in wanting to kill a man because of his stupidity. Abigail had not only saved her household, but her intelligence also made her so incredibly attractive to David that after her husband died, Abigail became one of David's first wives. I guess that even in biblical times a brainy woman could excite a man.

—

WE'VE ALREADY LEARNED in past chapters that women in ancient Greece were second-class citizens without many rights that today would be considered inherent for all human beings. For example, the ancient Greeks considered intelligence a manly characteristic, and yet, during these times, there were women who made groundbreaking intellectual contributions to society.

At the end of the seventh century BC, Sappho became the first female poet in Western literature. Although her love poems were addressed to women, she entertained relationships with men, as evidenced by the recounting of many legends about her life. These legends tell us that she was married to a man named Kerkylas, and yet she was passionately in love with the ferryman Phaon. Because this love was unrequited, she eventually threw herself off the Leucadian Cliffs. As most of her poems no longer exist, it's difficult for us to get a good sense of her intellectual talents. However, Plato admired her mind and bestowed on her the title of The Tenth Muse. This was a tremendous accolade coming from someone who thought poetry was a waste of time. As difficult as it is to pair Sappho with a specific romantic interest from the remnants of information written about her, there are numerous written accounts alluding to Sappho's intelligence, creating a spark that smoldered in many men's hearts.

The historical veracity of narratives about females in fifth century BC Athens continue to remain suspect because of fear that these accountings were mostly written by men. However, if we are to trust the words of recognized great thinkers such as Aristophanes, Plato, and Plutarch we will see that there was at least one woman, Aspasia, who earned respect and admiration from each of these three men. It was even suggested that she influenced Socrates's understanding of love, as noted in Plato's *The Symposium*.

Aspasia's intellect attracted the attention of Pericles, a great statesman and military leader of that time. Although they never married because Aspasia wasn't born in Athens, Pericles and Aspasia lived together and were inseparable. Pericles' great speeches were credited to the influence of Aspasia. He praised Aspasia's political wisdom for much of the achievements of this golden age of Athens, even though his critics condemned him for taking counsel from a woman. It's pretty clear that Pericles was looking for more than physical beauty in a mate, and Aspasia had a brain, and she knew how to use it to get her man.

―

MOST LOVE STORIES focus on a woman's beauty or sexuality. It's not easy to find examples of men so captivated by a woman's brain that a bond could be maintained with her just because of her intelligence. Nonetheless, the Medieval love story of Abelard and Heloise provides evidence that a man can still be enthralled by a woman when sex abates. Abelard met Heloise in 1115 when she was living with her uncle. She was known to be a brilliant scholar. Her uncle graciously permitted Abelard to tutor her, but Abelard had some decidedly prurient ideas about Heloise that had nothing to do with instruction in the classics. He seduced and married her, and she became pregnant. Her outraged uncle sent men to castrate Abelard. After this wicked deed was done,

Abelard decided to become a monk and then convinced Heloise to become a nun and enter a convent. Abelard may have felt that if he couldn't have Heloise then he'd make sure that no one else could, either. However, I'd like to think that he considered their love superior to bodily lust. The couple's writings to each other for the remainder of their lives were full of philosophical reflections on life and love. Their writings demonstrate a passionate love life devoid of carnality. Instead, their relationship was based on a fascination with each other's intellects. Abelard may have initially been attracted to Heloise because of her beauty, but ultimately his ardent feelings for her came from his admiration for her mind.

The Victorian era was a low point for the promotion of rights for women. Most families saw no point in educating women. Women from wealthy families were only taught the skills required to become a lady who, once married, would become the property of her husband. Lower-class women would be forced to work in the mills or factories to help support their families. It was an accepted belief that if a woman had any ideas at all, it was because she stole them from a man. This denial of female intellectualism created antagonism toward any woman who spoke out about issues of the day, and yet, despite this, there were a few women who made a name for themselves. One of these outspoken women was Florence Nightingale.

The "Lady with the Lamp" is an appellation that identified Florence Nightingale. She received the title because she would nurse wounded soldiers late at night. However, she was also a brilliant statistician and founder of modern nursing. Her brilliance led her to present statistics as pictures utilizing a polar area diagram. Until she revolutionized the field of nursing in the early nineteenth century, it was considered nothing but menial work. Her intellect was intriguing to many men, as evidenced by her receiving four proposals of marriage. She rejected them all, even though she enjoyed long-term relationships with some of the men. Nightingale was in a nine-year relationship with Richard Monkton Milnes, and yet, in the end, she also rejected his proposal of marriage. She said that she had a "moral . . . active nature that requires satisfaction and that I would not find in his life." It would be an understatement to say that Nightingale had a restless mind. She wasn't known for her wit or beauty, and was even known to have a harsh demeanor. Nevertheless, not many women can claim four proposals of marriage, so clearly, Nightingale's intelligence lit a spark of something in these men.

TODAY

Unfortunately, the twentieth century wasn't always that progressive a time for women's rights. A woman who declared herself as a feminist and political activist could suffer punitive consequences. Nonetheless, there were women who dedicated themselves to promoting equity for women.

Josephine Baker was a British advocate who worked tirelessly for suffrage, a woman's right to education, abolishing child prostitution, and stopping human trafficking. Her greatest efforts were directed at abolishing couverture, which was the blending of a woman's legal existence into that of her husband's. As was customary for women who lived during the early part of this century, Baker had very little formal education. Regardless of this deficiency, she was a prolific writer who also spoke several languages. She married George Butler, who was a scholar and cleric, mainly because she hoped to expand her education. His spiritual beliefs led him to the conclusion that men and women were equal, a scandalous concept during Victorian times. Once Baker's rhetoric became well-known, his own career suffered, and yet he treasured his wife's brilliance so much that he gladly took second place in importance in their lives. Baker's influence also was a major component in the repeal of the Contagious Disease Acts, which gave police the right to detain and forcefully conduct an internal examination on any woman suspected of prostitution. Baker was reviled and was socially isolated for speaking about such a taboo subject, and yet her husband never left her side and always supported the ideas of his smart wife.

When I think of other smart women of the twentieth century, Madeleine Albright and Ruth Bader Ginsberg immediately come to mind. Unfortunately, some of the men in these women's lives thought that being with an intelligent woman diminished their male status.

Madeleine Albright was the first female US secretary of state, a position which undoubtably required a good intellect, and yet as noted in her memoir, *Madam Secretary,* reporters covering the UN used to call her "Madeleine Half-Bright" as they didn't want to credit her expertise in an arena that was always an all-boys club. Her husband divorced her after many years of marriage, and her memoirs indicate that he was perhaps intimidated by her brains and success. He told Albright that he would dump his mistress and come home if he won the Pulitzer Prize. He didn't win. Her husband couldn't bear having her light shine brighter than his, even though Albright said that she would have given up her career to save her marriage. Ah, apparently, at least for women, sometimes love is blind.

Everyone feels insecure at times in a relationship. However, a person's strong character is demonstrated when they can put aside their insecurities to focus on the happiness of their partners.

The comprehensive biography, *Ruth Bader Ginsburg* by Jane Sherron De Hart, presents a startling contrast between the marital relationships of Ginsberg and Albright. Martin Ginsberg's devotion to his wife, Ruth, made him sparkle like the brightest star in the sky. Both Martin and Ruth attended Harvard Law School together. Although Martin didn't make the Harvard Law Review, Ruth did, and Martin made sure to spread the word of Ruth's success to everyone. Martin became a successful tax attorney, and yet he still used every opportunity to praise his wife's intellect. Ruth knew that Martin appreciated her intellect as she told their son, "Dad was the only boy who dated her who cared that she had a brain." This is quite a contrast to Madeleine Albright's husband's jealous reaction to Madeleine's brilliance. But not all men considered Ruth's brains attractive.

In Ruth's younger years, she was considered by some men an

oddity who was reaching above her gender status. In 1956, she was one of nine women at Harvard Law School. One day she and her female classmates were summoned into the dean's office and were questioned as to why they were occupying seats that should be filled by men. After graduation from law school, Ruth confidently applied for a clerkship with Supreme Court Justice Felix Frankfurter. She was turned down because Frankfurter said he wasn't ready to hire a woman. I guess he had the mindset of some of the old-school males of the 1950s who believed a woman's role was cooking, cleaning, and making babies, brain or no brain.

—

BY THE TWENTY-FIRST century, society had gotten to the point where, according to the National Student Clearinghouse Research Center, women accounted for 60 percent of all college students at the end of the 2021-2022 academic year. The pool of smart women for men to fish around in had exploded. Women were proud of their brains and were ready to challenge anyone who doubted their knowledge. There are so many exemplary examples of smart women that it is difficult to sufficiently narrow down my list of names. Therefore, I decided to focus on women who are most familiar to everyone. Some of them, like Hillary Clinton and Maria Shriver, became well-known because of their association with famous men, while Angela Merkel and Sheryl Sandberg had only themselves to thank for their amazing successes. Regardless of how they attained recognition, it is undeniable that these women possess superior intelligence.

Before becoming the first lady of the United States and then secretary of state, Hillary was an attorney who graduated from Yale Law School. The *National Law Journal* twice listed her as one of the most influential lawyers in America. Although being married to the president of the United States couldn't hurt someone's standing in the world, it's almost certain that she would have succeeded in reaching her goals on her own merits. She was elected to the US Senate and reached the pinnacle of her success in 2009 when she was appointed secretary of state by President Obama and became the first woman to become the presidential nominee for a major political party. Unfortunately, she hit a glass ceiling and lost the election to the demeaning and arguably sexist Republican candidate, Donald Trump.

During the early years of her relationship with her husband Bill, Hillary decided to temporarily bow to society's conventional ideas regarding acceptable women's behavior to help her husband succeed in his campaign. She even conformed to the conventional practice of using her husband's surname, but this deferential behavior was difficult for Hillary to maintain. Her confrontational style was off-putting to many women and men, and yet the aggressive use of her intellect was attractive to Bill.

As president, Bill suggested that he might give his wife a cabinet job, and although that never happened it was clear that his presidency would be a partnership with his wife. Hillary made it clear that although she could have stayed home, baked cookies, and had teas, she decided to fulfill her own lofty ambitions. Hillary always elicited strong emotions from people. Whether you loved or hated her, you have to admit that she was dedicated to pursuing her own career goals, and her husband was her greatest cheerleader once she entered the world of politics.

When Hillary became first lady, Bill publicly lauded her intelligence by giving her an office in the West Wing, since he believed that she needed to be with the other domestic policy advisers. Many acquaintances commented that part of the couple's attraction to each other was the regard they had for each other's intelligence. Bill summed up his admiration when he said of his wife that she was "the most qualified person to run for office in my lifetime, including me." It's interesting to note that most of Bill's alleged affairs were with women who held subordinate workplace positions. Perhaps his focus in these other relationships centered on something other than intelligence.

Not much has been revealed about German Chancellor Angela Merkel's two husbands other than that they were both bright men. Her second husband, Joachim Sauer, is described as being one of the top thirty theoretical chemists worldwide. Most people would probably blanch at the notion of engaging in a conversation with their husband about quantum chemistry, and yet Merkel received a doctorate degree in the subject. Consequently, she could certainly hold her own in any discourse. Without a doubt, her intelligence qualified her to become her country's first woman chancellor, and yet her intellect and strength repelled some men, especially those men who believed in the supremacy of the patriarchy.

Merkel had a tremendous fear of dogs. The people that she interacted with in the international community were aware of this fear. In 2007, Vladimir Putin brought his Labrador retriever to a press conference that he knew Merkel would be attending. She commented about his insensitivity to her phobia by saying, "I understand why he has to do this to prove he's a man—he's afraid of his own weakness." It would be difficult to find evidence that men were turned on by Merkel as she never projected any sensuality into her persona. Germans called her "Mutti for Mommy" because of her talent for caring for the German people. She downplayed her charisma when talking about herself.

French President Nicolas Sarkozy and Merkel often visited Toulouse together. The president told Merkel that the crowd was happy to see them. She responded to him, "Nicolas, I think compared to you, I am an energy-conserving lamp." Her modest choice of words underscores her deliberate, productive interaction with people, behavior that earned her *Time* magazine's title of the most powerful woman in the world. Although Merkel was never lauded for her physical appearance, she was constantly recognized for her intelligence.

It seems like the tech industry, like the higher echelons of politics, attracts men and women who take enormous pride in the development of their intellects. This is not to say that intellectuals are not attractive, yet many of its superstars at one time in their lives have been considered nerds. Bill Gates, once the richest man in the United States, would be considered by most people as the perfect definition of a computer nerd. It's not surprising that he would be attracted to smart women. Although he was no Lothario, he did have two long-term relationships with two women before he married Melinda. Both of his girlfriends were employed in the tech industry and Gate's comment that he and his first girlfriend looked alike probably meant that she wasn't a model.

When Bill met Melinda French she was also involved in tech as the product manager at Microsoft. She was considered a genius who promoted STEM education for women. She graduated valedictorian of her class in 1982. She received two bachelor's degrees in computer science and economics and went on to obtain her master's. Maybe one of the most telling comments about the relationship between Gates and Malinda French came from his second girlfriend, Ann Winblad, when she said about French, "I said she'd be a good match for him because she had intellectual stamina." After Gates and French were together a year, she walked into his room to discover him writing on a whiteboard the pros and cons of a marriage commitment. They were a nice looking but not glamorous couple, and neither one of them exuded sensual vibes. Nonetheless, there was something about French that intrigued Gates, and based on her accomplishments I'd bet that intelligence was the top item listed on the pro side of that whiteboard. Unfortunately, it looks like Gates, just like Bill Clinton, was also beguiled by something other than intelligence in his attraction to women. French's intelligence never diminished, and yet Gates engaged in an affair with an employee. This transgression, combined with his acquaintance with sex offender Jeffrey Epstein, suggests that maybe Gates first pro on the whiteboard should have been sex.

THERE'S AN UNDENIABLE status to being the COO of Facebook (Meta), and being the first COO was even more impressive, especially if you are a woman. In 2008, Sheryl Sandberg became that woman. She attributed much of her success to the support of her second husband, David Goldberg, who exuded confidence and had achieved powerful leadership positions and vast wealth. He had walked away from a leadership position at Launch Media with a fifteen-million-dollar exit bonus and then became the CEO of Survey Monkey. Yet, Goldberg happily maintained an unassuming demeanor and, instead, at every opportunity, lavished praise on his wife's intelligence. When Sandberg was considering a job at Facebook, he told her to ask for more money as he estimated her abilities at the highest level. He was clearly a man who was enamored with his wife's intelligence. In Sandberg's hit book, *Lean In*, she advises women to find a man "who thinks women should be smart, opinionated and ambitious." She found this man in Goldberg.

Perhaps Maria Shriver should have followed Sandberg's advice before she entered a relationship with Arnold Schwarzenegger. Shriver's mother, Eunice Kennedy Shriver, encouraged her daughter to engage in intellectual pursuits because, she admonished, that brains were more important than beauty. Maria Shriver took her mother's advice seriously and focused her energies on pursuing a career in journalism, anchoring *CBS News*, *NBC News*, the *Today Show*, and acting as a correspondent for *Dateline*. But then she met Arnold Schwarzenegger and Maria's Shriver's ambitions were cut short when he ran for governor of California. She gave up her career and focused her time on helping Arnold Schwarzenegger get elected. Her sacrifice didn't prevent her husband from committing many infidelities, culminating with having a child with another woman.

Schwarzenegger didn't attempt to hide his feelings about the basis for his initial attraction to Shriver. When he was first introduced to her mother Eunice, he told her, "Your daughter has a great body." Conceivably, he believed that he was giving Shriver a great compliment. The fact that Shriver was a Kennedy might also have enhanced

Shriver's desirability in Schwarzenegger's eyes as he might have been harboring political aspirations for quite some time. Although we really can't look into a person's heart, based on Schwarzenegger's very public sexual predilections, it doesn't seem farfetched to surmise that it wasn't only Shriver's mind that prompted Schwarzenegger to pursue a relationship with her.

Now that you've read about so many smart women, can you tell me why you think that the men in their lives had such different reactions to their intelligence? Were the men full of, or lacking in self-confidence? Did their upbringing or societal norms influence their reactions to these women? Or can you think of something else?

This is a perfect time to look at our surveys to see if any of our respondents can help us with these questions and the question, "Do smart women turn you on or off?"

MEN'S RESPONSES

RESPONSE	PERCENTAGE
On	62
Off	28
It Depends	10

Our male respondents were quite expressive in their comments. It was difficult to pick just a few out of the many interesting ones, but here is what I chose.

- "I would say they turn me on in a primal way."
- "On, because I am smart."
- "It depends on how they show their smartness. Women who feel they need to show it off . . . are not attractive."
- "Smart women tend to be know-it-all showoffs who lash males as toxic."

- "On. I want someone who will engage me . . . I don't get that from an idiot."
- "On, beauty fades."
- "On, stupidity's bestiality."
- "Smart is not sexy."
- "On, my wife isn't particularly intellectual, and it gets a bit frustrating at times."

It's a good thing that the survey was anonymous, or the last respondent might have a bit of explaining to do to his wife. Interestingly, some of the respondents didn't actually object to intelligence in a mate as long as the mate didn't flaunt their intelligence.

The female respondents' answers were almost evenly divided between Yes, No and It Depends. Most of the women's comments reflect their thoughts that the men's answers were dependent on the emotional security level of the male respondent.

WOMEN'S RESPONSES

RESPONSES	PERCENTAGE
On	33
Off	34
It depends	33

A few of the female respondents' comments seem to disparage men's characters, classifying men who are turned off by smart women as feeling intimidated, threatened or being immature, or stupid.

- "Only turns off the dumb ones."
- "Off, because they might feel that they are not that smart."
- "Off, because men like to be dominant and they like girls that are a little silly."

- "On, they turn on confident men and scare away the others."
- "Off, smart women petrify men."
- "On, no one wants a bimbo."
- "Smart women can turn men on, so long as they aren't smarter than men. Smart women are appealing but women who are TOO smart make men feel inferior."
- "The idea of a smart woman is sexy, the reality of a woman smarter than themselves is often harder for them to stomach."
- "Depends on the level of maturity and character. Worthwhile men should find it appealing, immature ones may be intimidated and find it easier to manipulate, control and impress a stupid person."

A common thread in both the female and male respondent's answers to this survey question is that a man might be turned on by a smart woman as long as she is not smarter than him. But what happens if a woman is not only smart, but also financially supports or earns more than the man in her life? Keep on reading, and together, we'll discover how a man reacts to a woman being the breadwinner in the relationship.

CHAPTER 6

SHE'S GOT THE MONEY, HONEY; BUT WHO WEARS THE PANTS?

The Broadway musical *Cabaret's* homage to the glories of money in the song "Money" underscores the general assumption that men make the money and women take it. The lyrics, "money makes the world go around," pointedly makes this clear. In the play the ensemble joyfully sings that if you need a companion and you have money, then you can just ring for the maid, the implication being that this maid will do more than scrub your bathroom floor.

Many of the musical's women who worked at the Kit Kat club used their sexuality as part of their act and dutifully strutted their stuff to attract a sugar daddy. The concept of a beautiful woman capturing a wealthy man is repeated many times in literature and the theater. However, the reverse situation is rarely depicted in the creative arts—unless the man is a gigolo. Presumably, this might be because creative arts often imitate life and the image of a *sugar mommy* isn't attractive to most men, or is it? Maybe Jim, Noah, or Buddy can help us discover whether men feel comfortable being financially supported by a woman, or by her earning more than he does.

Jim thought it was inconceivable that his wife would ever financially support him or earn more than him as she had begun her career very late in life. It took some time, but she did catch up to him. Jim had secretly hoped that his wife's income from her new job would increase enough so they could hire a maid, and he would no longer have to help with the household chores. He also wanted to take more luxurious vacations. He said to Noah and Buddy, "I guess that

I'd selfishly enjoy reaping the benefits of the extra income. However, I'm not sure if I would be willing to give up the sense of control and power I get from everyone in the family depending on me to take care of them. In other words, I'm not willing to give up my role as chief breadwinner in the family."

—

I WONDER HOW many of you reading Jim's words can recall the moment that you realized the importance of money in your life. For me, that moment happened when I was fifteen years old. I remember asking my mother for money to go see a movie with my friends. My mother told me that she didn't like one of my friends, so she'd only give me the money if that friend also wasn't going to the movie. Even at that young age, I realized that money equaled control and power. Jim's insecurity about maintaining control makes it unlikely that he would ever be comfortable with a woman financially supporting him.

"Wow man," said Buddy. "Who would have thought that I'd hold the enlightened view about a woman earning more money than her partner or even supporting him? I don't know why Jim doesn't see this scenario as more than a way to provide small perks for the family. I'd take full advantage of not having to bring home the bacon. I can imagine myself sleeping late while wifey rushes off to catch the train to work, and then, when I leisurely get out of bed, I'd check the sports schedule to see what's on that day. Later that night I'd look forward to exercising some conjugal rights in bed with my wife."

After hanging out with Buddy for many years, Jim and Noah didn't think that anything Buddy said would shock them, but this latest utterance astonished them. Buddy then says, "Why are you guys looking at me like you've never seen me before? I am totally secure in my dominance over the female gender, so if a woman wants to support me I'd gladly let her. I'm worth it. Women were created to serve men, so why shouldn't a woman use her money to make me happy? After all, look at the gift that I'm giving her just by letting her be with me. I don't need money to feel powerful or in control because those two traits already define who I am." It looks like Buddy has no problem with a woman being the breadwinner in a relationship as long as he can be her sugar baby.

Noah's head is ready to explode as he contemplates everything that Buddy has just said. He wonders how Buddy could aspire to basically become a kept man. Noah prides himself on his intellect and believes that the worth of a man is not based on how much money he has in his pocket, but on how much wisdom that he has in his head. That wisdom isn't affected because or whether a woman earns more than him or supports him. Even if his partner was a billionaire, he would still pursue his career goals. He's repelled by Buddy's concept of life without a purpose. He tells his friends, "Some of the world's most powerful men used only their brains to achieve greatness. For example, the name Machiavelli is associated with deceit and treachery. However, it is undeniable that he was the first political writer to separate politics from morality and to describe the political world as it was, rather than what people hoped it would be. His philosophy had a profound impact on leaders, which has lasted throughout the ages. As a result, Machiavelli became one of the most influential men of his time because of his intellect. I'm not saying that I consider myself on a level with Machiavelli, but as long as I can think then I'll never be intimidated by someone having more money than me. I don't want a woman to want me because I can support her, and I certainly don't care what she brings home in her paycheck. We'll throw all our money together in a pot and then sit around with a good glass of wine and read Proust together. I guess this means that, yes, I'm comfortable with a woman supporting me or making more money than I make."

Who would ever think that Noah and Buddy would share the same sentiment about relationships between men and women even though Buddy's and Noah's reasoning behind their sentiment is not even close to being in the same ballpark?

Money has always played an important role in people's lives. Wars are fought to gain another country's riches and relationships are made and broken because of it. Before money was the official medium of exchange, bartering was common. Bartering was using the exchange of goods or services in the place of money. However, bartering had many limitations, so it was eventually replaced by money. There have been many forms of money throughout history before it morphed into what we use today and regardless of its form, money has always been equated with power.

Different countries have different currencies, but the goal is always the same, and that is to get lots of it. This thirst for wealth beckons stories lauding the latest billionaire's net worth or their green-eyed envy over a celebrity's twenty-seven-million-dollar home. How can men cast aside society's mindset that the worth of a man depends on how much money he has, and that shames him if he is not the breadwinner in his home? Perhaps we'll get some hints to help us answer this question in the next section when we explore how men of past generations reacted to this doctrine.

YESTERDAY

Many of us have heard the biblical story of Joanna, Mary Magdalene, and Susanna, the three women who attended to the tomb of Jesus Christ in anticipation of his resurrection. If a Christian, you'll either nod in fond recognition of this cherished story from your childhood Christian religious education, or you'll guffaw at my reference to what you consider a fictional fable. Regardless of your ideology, the Bible provides riveting examples of both exemplary and dishonorable human behavior. Many of these stories are embellished with sensational images of things like parting seas and swarms of locusts. However, there are other narratives that focus on less dramatic acts, such as the patronage provided to Jesus by Joanna, Mary, and Susanna. These three women were financially independent and used their wealth to support Jesus as he and the twelve Apostles went on their pilgrimage. According to the Bible, Jesus was the son of God, so he certainly didn't need the women's money. Perhaps the scribes wrote this tale to illustrate that even great men could depend on a woman for their financial stability without losing masculinity or status.

Queen Berenice of Celicia, born in the fourth century, never had a problem attracting men and was a widow twice by the time she was twenty. She was a woman of great wealth and power, initially as a princess of Judea and then, after marrying King Herod, she became a queen. After Herod died, Berenice was again part of the dating market. Although Berenice was beautiful, King Polemon found her wealth a greater attraction. He wanted to marry Berenice to use her money to run his kingdom. She agreed to marry him only if he converted to Judaism and underwent circumcision, which he did. Nevertheless, Berenice left Polemon shortly after their marriage and returned to live with her brother Agrippa II. We must assume that Polemon was very comfortable with Berenice supporting him since he willingly altered what most men consider a favorite part of their body in exchange for her hand in marriage and access to her fortune.

Many men of the Bible either were apparently so secure in their tremendous power over women that they were willing to give up some control for financial gain, or on the other hand, they had such inflated egos that they truly believed they were the superior gender. To them, it was a woman's obligation to bestow on men all of their worldly goods as well as sexual favors.

The relationship between Mark Anthony and Cleopatra is the subject of many movies and books. This first century couple used their individual resources to challenge the power dynamics of ancient Rome. Mark Anthony was a renowned military strategist who loved many women and equally loved to gamble. His gambling wasn't always successful, so he would never turn his nose down to a woman who could help him fill his pockets with money and provide him with the resources needed for him to succeed with his military campaigns.

Cleopatra was the queen of Egypt. Historians note her worth (in current dollars) at ninety-five billion or more. She had all the money that she would ever need, and yet she still needed help to protect her crown and Egypt's independence. Anthony and Cleopatra exemplify the perfect symbiotic relationship. Each helped each other achieve their goals. Cleopatra's wealth was an important part of the allure that attracted Mark Anthony to her. He never lost any of his power because she shared her riches with him. We can gather that Mark Anthony was jubilant by Cleopatra's affluence.

—

THE SIXTH CENTURY in China wasn't a good time for women's rights, and yet it was ruled by Empress Wu, one of the richest women in history. Wu controlled what today would be equal to sixteen trillion dollars in assets. She definitely would do anything to maintain her power, even supposedly murdering one of her children and disposing of her sons, who were emperors, so that she could take their place. Despite being notoriously ruthless, she managed to attract two husbands and many lovers and used her wealth to achieve all her goals. Apparently, her second husband, Emperor Gaozong, was so enamored of her that when he became sickly, he handed his kingdom to her for twenty-three years and let her do whatever she wished with it. Gaozong trusted her enough that when his sight failed, he had Empress Wu read reports to him, not knowing that she would be altering the reports to tell him what she wanted him to hear. She had beauty, intelligence, and fortune, and men flocked to her to savor these attributes.

The story of Catherine the Great of Russia underscores the fact that many men can be comfortable and possibly ecstatically excited about the thought of a woman having more money than they have as long as it's being shared with them. Catherine was a penniless Russian princess who grew up in the eighteenth century. Although she was not considered beautiful, her family on her mother's side provided her with the connections to marry a man who was in the line of succession to become the Russian czar. Unfortunately, this man, Peter III, was a psychotic alcoholic. Catherine may have been lacking in beauty, but she had more than an abundant amount of guile and intelligence. Her marriage was a sham, and although she produced three children it was said that none of them was an offspring from Peter's seed. Six months after Peter was named czar, Catherine mounted a coup and Peter was overthrown. He was assassinated six days later, and some would say that his death was ordered by Catherine.

Catherine now had all the power and wealth of Russia, and she used much of it to make her many lovers happy, and her lovers were indeed very happy. During their relationships with Catherine, and even after they ended, these men received titles, land, palaces, and indentured servants. She even threw the might of the Russian military behind the efforts of her lover Poniatowski to become the King of Poland. Catherine kept publicly distributing her assets to her lovers. As she got older her lovers got younger and younger and became known as Catherine's "kept girls." By all accounts, men vied to be one of these kept girls; however, we can't be sure if they ever felt a twinge of discomfort at Catherine's lavish coddling. If so, they never refused.

TODAY

Sometimes a man can become too comfortable taking money from a woman, especially if that woman is so flattered by a man's attentions that she becomes duped by it. The relationship of Liliane Bettencourt and Francois-Marie Banier could be the basis for a thrilling mystery. However, to the family of this deceased L'Oréal scion, the actual events would more appropriately be viewed as a horror story. At the time of her death in 2017, Bettencourt was the richest woman in the world. She loved parties and having fun and, in her later years, decided that her husband had become boring and too staid for her taste. Bettencourt then met the celebrity photographer Francois-Marie Banier, who was only too happy to show Bettencourt a good time in exchange for some trinkets.

Over several years, those trinkets added up to more than a billion euros in gifts, including real estate, a signed art collection worth one hundred million euros, a private island in the Seychelles and 92 percent of her estate. Luckily, Bettencourt had a loyal butler who recorded some of Francois's sweet talk soliciting these gifts from Bettencourt. Bettencourt's family then got involved and in 2014 a court declared Liliane unable to handle her affairs, and her daughter was appointed guardian of her fortune. Francoise might have enjoyed spending Bettencourt's fortune, but it's doubtful that he enjoyed the three-year prison term that he was given in 2015 for the crime. In some cases, a man can be too comfortable benefiting from a woman's riches.

Being married to the richest person in the Netherlands could prompt a man to lean back and enjoy his wife's fortune. But aside from enjoying all the free beer that he could drink, this wasn't the case for Michael de Carvalho, the husband of Charlene de Carvalho-Heineken, the sole heir to the Heineken fortune. He married Heineken with the full knowledge that upon the death of her father she would inherit a 25 percent controlling interest in the world's second-largest brewer. If we look at Michael's background, we realize that throughout his life he snubbed money in exchange for doing what he loved. After dropping out of Harvard to pursue his dreams and incurring his parents' wrath, Michael became a three-time Olympian.

Even though they cut him off, Michael managed to survive, and after returning to school and receiving his Harvard MBA, he became a successful investment banker. He then married Heineken in 1983, and until her father died in 2002, her only wealth was a single share of Heineken stock, which at the time was worth only thirty-three dollars. Michael's attitude toward Heineken's potential windfall inheritance is best captured in what Heineken's dad said about Michael: "He's not interested in Heineken for her money." The fact that Michael bragged that he and his wife drove Volkswagens punctuated his minimalist outlook. It's undeniable that Heineken's net worth in 2022 of more than fifteen billion dollars could have been intimidating to some people around her, but it's clear from reading about Michael that he was not one of those people.

YOU HAVE TO be really rich, famous, infamous, or both, to be recognized by your first name only. The names Madonna, Cher, Prince, Elvis, Bono, and Hitler come to mind. Very few people don't recognize Oprah. She is a multimedia executive, actress, writer, producer, talk show host, philanthropist and, as of 2022, the richest self-made Black woman in America. All of this might make a potential romantic partner a bit intimated but Stedman Graham, her boyfriend of thirty-seven years, would disagree. When asked about their relationship in an interview he said, "I'm not threatened by her fame or her success or her money or all of that. That's who she is. It doesn't have anything to do with how I define myself." It probably helps that he's an author of more than ten bestselling books and a successful business owner with a net worth of over ten million dollars. Oprah's words, "Lots of people want to ride with you in the limo, but what you want is someone who will take the bus with you when the limo breaks down," indicate that she wasn't looking for a man who was a fortune hunter. Do you think that the dynamic of their relationship would change, and his feelings would be different if he were a minimum-wage earner doing manual labor?

Most of us aren't written about in history books or command vast fortunes and yet our finances play a prominent role in how we think about ourselves. Our survey's male respondents resoundingly answered *yes* to the question, "Would you feel comfortable with a woman financially supporting you, and/or if your partner earned more than you?"

MEN'S RESPONSES

RESPONSES	PERCENTAGE
Yes	73
No	24
Don't know	3

It's interesting to note that some of the men responding yes to our question chose to qualify their answers. They wanted to make it clear that although they would be comfortable with their female partner making more than they did, this comfort didn't extend to her supporting him. Some of the men's comments were quite complex and revealed more than a simple yes or no answer. Here are some of their comments:

- "I would be okay with it, as long as she is not overworking and throws it in my face."
- "Yes, if a woman is more financially stable than me it would feel somewhat emasculating. However, there would be some pride and admiration in her success."
- "No, I am too prideful for anyone to support me financially."
- "No, I have what some would call foolish male pride."
- "Yes, because I'm comfortable in my own capabilities not to feel threatened."
- "No, I have no rationale for this."
- "I'd be okay if she earned more, just not financially supporting me. I'm old school."

These comments, like many of the others included in the survey, suggest that pride is a big issue in a man's comfort level regarding a woman's financial support in a relationship. Surprisingly, the female respondents' answers were almost diametrically opposed to the answers that they thought were given by the men.

WOMEN'S RESPONSES

RESPONSES	PERCENTAGE
Yes	28
No	58
Depends on the man and/or circumstances	14

Many of the women's comments when referencing the men's answers are tinged with sarcasm or humor. What do you think they mean? Let's take a look at them.

- "Twenty-five percent of the men would be comfortable because they could be lazy and get taken care of."
- "No, because men have to feel superior to women."
- "Smart men and dumb men, yes. Guys in the middle? No, they see it as an affront to their own power and manliness."
- "No, most men have ego issues."
- "No, because it is not macho."
- "I've supported a few. They weren't comfortable but they didn't stop me."
- "Yes, easy street."
- "Most guys have problems when a woman earns more than they do. I don't know why. Maybe something falls off."

I think that the last comment would cause many men to cringe at the image portrayed, but it's certainly a colorful representation of male emasculation. The survey has given us a good idea about how men feel about women having greater financial resources in a relationship. Now it's time to look to see if men think that women place more importance on a man's financial status or his appearance.

CHAPTER 7

WHAT TURNS WOMEN ON?
A DREAMY SMILE OR A BMW?

LET ME SHARE with you the image that immediately pops into my head when I think about this question. There are a group of people standing together at a party. One of the men is a dead ringer for Brad Pitt. He's got the face, body, and sex appeal, but from the looks of his clothes he doesn't have any money. There is another man at the party who seems to be getting all the attention of the group and yet even his mother would probably be hard-pressed to call him handsome. What is there about this man that commands the respect and attention of the group? Is it because everyone knows that he is rich? If I was at this party, can you guess which man I would be most interested in dating? How about you?

Is it possible that men judge the importance women place on a man's financial status and appearance based on their self-image? A homely man with a lot of money might think that he's not attractive to women because of his looks, while an attractive guy might blame his failure to establish a relationship with a woman on his poor economic status. These assumptions might be correct, but many times there are other underlying reasons behind a woman's attraction to a man. In an attempt to stack the deck in favor of money versus appearance, we can all tell stories about women who have dated physically grotesque, affluent men. However, are these women actually attracted to these men or simply *with* them? Perhaps our trio of friends can shed some light on our questions.

IT'S ANOTHER NIGHT at the bar and Jim, Buddy, and Noah settle in with fresh drinks as they prepare themselves for a discussion of whether women place more importance on a man's financial status or his appearance.

Jim likes to think of himself as the *total package* when it comes to what he can offer a woman. He considers himself handsome and fit. He believes that he has a captivating personality and lots of money. Listening to him speak, someone might consider him an egomaniac, and yet there is a side to him that emanates sweetness and empathy. Jim unabashedly blurts out, "I don't think that I'm conceited when I say that if I got divorced tomorrow there would probably be a line of women outside my door wanting to date me. I've worked diligently all of my life to stay in shape. I watch what I eat, practice good hygiene, and exercise several times a week. I keep up on the latest cultural trends so I can contribute to conversations in a stimulating way. My wealth wasn't given to me. From the time that I was a young boy, I created opportunities to make money. At the age of fifteen, I was detailing people's Lamborghinis in my parent's driveway for one hundred and twenty-five per car. It follows that since I worked hard to become the man that I am today, I'm not ashamed to admit that I consider myself a catch. If I were back on the single's scene a woman dating me wouldn't have to decide whether my wealth or appearance was most important. If a woman was lucky enough to get me, she would get it all."

Buddy teases, "You make perfect sense, Jim. Your wife should consider herself a blessed woman to have a man like you, especially because of your self-deprecating personality. But how do men like me, who aren't financial titans or have classically good looks, attract women? As I've mentioned before, I've always been lucky in my ability to charm women, and I think that the reason for this is that people interpret differently the meaning of the word appearance."

Buddy is definitely on to something; not everyone sees beauty in the same way. The actor Johnny Depp has been celebrated for his perfectly symmetrical face and was twice named the sexiest man alive. He's featured in the fantasies of women of all ages because of his beauty and smoldering temperament. In 2022, Dior renewed his contract to represent the face of its Sauvage perfume. Johnny's masculinity matches the raw wildness of the ad. He's depicted burying his jewelry in the desert as a pack of wolves surround him. The ad fades with him soulfully staring into the camera. You'd think that most women would agree that Johnny is a magnificent specimen, and yet there are many women who think he's a sleazy, depraved degenerate. By contrast, George Clooney's old-time Hollywood, good-guy looks present a significant contrast to Johnny's appearance, and yet both of them appeal to different women. Is Buddy correct when he infers that there is no universal gauge of good looks?

Buddy tells his friends, "Charisma is a trait that some men have, and others can never get. I'm happy to say that I've been told that when I turn on the charm that I'm irresistible. I don't have to spend hours in front of the mirror grooming because I know how to make a woman feel as if she's the most beautiful person in the world. When she looks at me she might not see George or Johnny, but she'll see someone who makes her feel special, and then I'll become special." Jim and Noah are amazed that Buddy sounds so unlike his usual caveman self. Buddy continues. "Let me end by saying that even if a man is unattractive or poor, he can still get a woman if he knows how to manipulate her." Buddy has apparently found a way to deal with his lack of wealth and good looks and, as reprehensible as his technique may be, it seems to work for him.

Although Noah isn't made of money, he manages to live a comfortable life. He has a nice apartment in a good section of the city, regularly attends the theater and symphony, and eats at upscale restaurants. However, he doesn't have an eighth of Jim's money and, consequently, doubts that any woman would want him. As far as his physical features, he would rate himself as pleasant looking. He believes that women find him alluring because of his intellect, which contributes to his overall appearance. He carries himself almost regally as he believes that he can offer a woman much more than she could obtain from a man with just a lot of money. His *wealth* consists of a vast accumulation of knowledge. He explains to Jim and Buddy, "Like Jim, I've spent a lot of time working on improving myself. When a woman meets me, she will walk away impressed with my mastery of a variety of topics and want to spend more time with me. I agree with Buddy that appearance is a lot more than an attractive face or buff body. You can make money, but you can also lose it. If who you are is based on something that is so ephemeral, then maybe you shouldn't base your desirability on financial worth. Knowledge is a more important thing to seek as you'll never lose it once it's gotten."

Our three men sound almost philosophical in their views about whether women are more attracted to wealthy or good-looking men. Let's learn if their observations match up with the behavior of men of yesterday and today.

YESTERDAY

The Bible is filled with stories about women who married extremely wealthy men. However, it's important to consider whether these marriages were a woman's choice or an arranged marriage in which her family would accumulate wealth, power, and political status. On the other hand, although we already mentioned the story of Abigail in our chapter on a woman's intelligence, I'll mention her and her partner again as it demonstrates that love matches did occur.

The story of Abigail and David illustrates the lure of beauty in a relationship. Abigail's husband was known for being brutish and mean. The *Aggadah* (rabbinic Jewish texts) treats Abigail as being one of the four most beautiful women in Jewish history. King David wasn't yet a rich king when he met Abigail. However, he was a dashing warrior and was seen as a kind of very handsome Robin Hood. Even the prophet Samuel acknowledged his beauty, saying David had "beautiful eyes and was handsome." Is it possible that Abigail married David because of his looks?

The results become very speculative when I attempt to get a more definitive answer as to whether women in biblical times put more importance on a man's wealth or looks. The Bible puts much emphasis on a woman's beauty yet barely recognizes male beauty. When male beauty is acknowledged it is usually followed by unpleasant events. Absalom was the third son of King David and was renowned for his beauty but never married. Strangely enough, the Bible doesn't mention his romantic relationships and yet it states that Absalom had three sons and one daughter, so we can speculate that some women must have liked him. However, it's unlikely that his personality made him attractive, as his behavior is described as treacherous. He killed his half-brother, had sexual relations with his father's concubines, and even plotted to kill his father. Absalom loved royal pretensions such as having fifty men run before him when he rode in his magnificent chariot and yet his actual wealth was rarely mentioned.

The Bible describes Absalom as the handsomest man in the kingdom stating, "He was flawless from head to foot" (2 Samuel 14:25, NLT). He was particularly proud of his long hair that he cut only once a year. Unfortunately, his pride and joy got caught in an oak tree when he was in battle, and Joab easily killed him. Maybe Absalom's vanity was the basis for the saying, "Pride goes before destruction, a haughty spirit before a fall."

Another biblical character who was praised for one of his physical attributes was Samson. Although most people assume that he was muscular, the only thing actually mentioned about his physical appearance in the Bible was his hair, which was credited as the source of his great strength. This hair is the focus of the famous story of Samson and Delilah. Samson was a real man's man. He killed a lion with his bare hands and destroyed an entire philistine army with just the jawbone of an ass. Yet, despite these superhero talents, Delilah chose to betray him for a few pieces of silver by cutting his hair and making him lose his strength. I guess women will sometimes do reprehensible things for money, regardless of the magnificent attractiveness of the man they're betraying.

There was possibly only one man in the Bible who was described as having it all, and that was King Solomon. His impressive looks were raved about in comments about him, such as "How handsome you are, my love. How delightful our bed is lush with foliage" (Song of Songs 1:16). It's hard to dispute a man's attractiveness when women write sonnets to him praising his good looks. In addition, his fortune at that time was noted as more than three trillion dollars. I guess that his more than seven hundred wives got the whole package when they accepted the king's marriage proposals.

Most women don't want to share their man with other wives, no matter how handsome or wealthy. As we've learned, although there were a few exceptions, the average woman living in biblical times usually had little choice in picking her male partner. Once married, wives must have fretted that they would be cast aside for a concubine. Regardless of what attracted a woman to a man, in the end the man held all the cards.

Ironically, women living in hunter-gatherer societies held great positions of power as their living group depended on them to provide sustenance. Men were charged with bringing home only meat, but the primitive tools that they used made their success very iffy. It's amusing to imagine a bunch of men hungrily awaiting the return of their women from their latest food gathering quests. Whatever food was found was shared with the group, and therefore a man's value didn't hinge on whether he was rich or poor. However, strong men were better hunters, making them more desirable as a mate. As Buddy suggested, there are many understandings of what constitutes someone's appearance. A strong man's big biceps would certainly be considered attractive to a woman if it meant that she would get better supplies of meat.

Despite the significant contributions of women to horticultural societies, the advent of plow agriculture shifted the dynamics of labor. The physical demands of plowing required strength, typically attributed to men, diminishing the importance of women in providing sustenance. As a result, a woman now needed to totally rely on a man to provide for her. Could it be that this evolutionary adaptiveness is causative in whether a woman placed more importance on a man's wealth or appearance?

—

WOMEN IN BIBLICAL and prehistoric times had it really easy compared to the lives of women of the Classical Greek period. It was thought that only an invisible Greek woman was a respectable one. She was secluded from the world and was rarely permitted to leave her house. By the age of fourteen her father had married her off to a man at least twice her age. There was never consideration of whether she was attracted to her potential mate. Most women's families gave them dowries to cover their expenses throughout their marriage. This dowry meant that it was the woman—not the man—who was prized for her financial riches. In a sense, it was more beneficial that a woman marry a man of modest means as it meant that she would be less sequestered.

There were no slaves in humble households, so wives had more work to do. Yet because of their labors, wives could get out of the house even if it was just to go to the wells for water and to sell their handmade goods and agricultural products. Marrying a poorer man gave a woman some freedom from sequestration. Since money was not a top consideration, the lure of a handsome man was extremely compelling. Most women, regardless of their means, had little opportunity for social interaction. Despite their being almost hermetically sealed off from the outside world, they made the most of the few opportunities to indulge their sexual appetites with someone with whom they had a physical attraction. Bizarrely, the ideal venue for meeting this potential lover was at a funeral. We have to assume that these adulterous affairs were based on a man's good looks, as there was little chance of the couple engaging in a soul-searching conversation. Both participants in the affair had much to lose. A husband could legally kill his wife's lover, and the wife would be automatically divorced and prohibited from participating in religious ceremonies. In the end, it appears that some women in Classical Greek times found the enticement of being with a handsome man a powerful enough incentive to risk possible severe punishment.

From what can be gathered from historical accounts, the accumulation of wealth was highly praised during Roman classical times as an important way to establish oneself in society. Occasionally, a woman was lucky enough to get a mate who was both wealthy and handsome. This was the case in the marriage of Amelia Tertia. Amelia married Scipio Africanus who, according to the Roman historian Levy, was considered the handsomest man of the classical Roman period. Tertia was known for ostentatious displays of the wealth that she shared with Scipio. She was even willing to conceal her husband's affair with one of their slave girls in order to continue enjoying Scipio's fortune. She might have appreciated his good looks but couldn't live without his money.

Each generation has its own perception of beauty. Men in Victorian times were lauded if they had delicate features with long-flowing hair. Lord Alfred Tennyson perfectly fits this description. He was regarded as a romantic and sentimental figure because of his celebrated poetry. Some of his phrases such as, "Tis better to have loved and lost, than never to have loved at all," have become commonplace in the English language. His wife, Emily, also was a poet. Emily and Alfred dated for thirteen years until Emily's father felt that Alfred was earning enough to support his daughter. Emily finally married Alfred at the age of thirty-seven. We can rule out wealth as a basis for Emily's attraction to Alfred. Instead, it was apparently his long-flowing locks that captivated her.

Society sets norms that influence role expectations for both men and women. In the Victorian age, all women who were born above the level of poverty were prohibited from working outside of the home. This meant that marriage to a man of means was necessary if they were to have a good life. The ideal man had to demonstrate that he had enough economic success to support a household and protect his family. An unmarried man was a failure as a man because he couldn't fulfill his duties in life. A woman's role in life was to take care of her family and household so she needed a man with resources to accomplish her goals.

There are always outliers in every generation. The renowned Victorian poet Elizabeth Barrett was one of them. She grew up in a twenty-bedroom mansion and because of her fragile health was a bit of a recluse. Her family's wealth guaranteed that she would never need a man to support her financially. Robert Browning was also a poet but never attained the literary status of Elizabeth. He was the son of a bank clerk who lived a modest lifestyle. Although Elizabeth's father considered Robert a fortune hunter, Elizabeth was determined to marry Robert regardless of his financial status. They eloped, and Elizabeth's father never spoke to her again. Whether Elizabeth was attracted to Robert's looks or personality, it seems clear that money wasn't the draw. Her eloquent words expressed this love, "I love thee with the breath, smiles, tears, of all my life; . . . I shall love thee better after death" (How do I love thee? Sonnet 43).

TODAY

The end of World War 1 brought many changes in the perception of male and female roles in society. While men served in the military, women were employed in jobs that were traditionally filled by men. When the war ended, these women were unwilling to return to the Victorian dictate that a woman must be subordinate to a man. This *new woman* expected to have the same economic and political rights as a man. Men returning home from the war struggled to balance charm and magnetism with his ability to provide for his family. The modern male became fixated on vanity and worked on his neglected social skills. The popular song, "Dapper Dan, The Sheik of Alabam," epitomized the life of the party man in its lyrics, "I ain't handsome, I ain't sweet, I'm the ladies' man Dapper Dan from Dixieland. I've got a brand of lovin' that can't be beat." Maybe Buddy was correct when he said a man's appearance was more than his good looks. However, the extravagant lifestyle of the flapper meant that there was still a significant emphasis on the importance of wealth in the 1920s.

Perhaps the best chroniclers of a generation are its authors, and the twentieth century yielded some of the most outstanding writers of any age. The epigraph from *The Great Gatsby* by F. Scott Fitzgerald succinctly sets the stage for a woman's expectations for her lover in the exhortation to a man to "Wear the gold hat" to impress his lover. Taking clues from his female peers, Fitzgerald created a world in which the female protagonist, Daisy, equally craves money and sex from her male partners. Gatsby recognizes that Daisy is a person of wealth and class and remarks about her that, "Her voice is full of money." So, he makes it his business to accumulate enough money to impress her. Daisy begins an affair with Gatsby only after she is given a tour of his mansion and becomes assured of his great wealth. However, she eventually leaves him because he is not as aristocratic or as wealthy as her husband, Tom.

In the 1920s, women were engaged in a tug of war over wealth versus good looks when judging a man's attractiveness. This dichotomy is clearly illustrated in Eugene O'Neill's play, *Strange Interlude*. Again, the playwright has based his perspective on observing women's behavior in the world in which he lived. The main character, Nina, is attracted to three different men—her husband, lover, and male childhood friend. The play centers on Nina's elusive search for love and her belief that each of the men in her life can give her different things. O'Neill captured the conundrum between Nina's desire for passion based on a man's appearance versus his financial status. She chose to have both as portrayed in the play. Perhaps it is as simple as that; most women aspire to have a male partner with both attributes.

AT THE END of the roaring 1920s, people were ready to usher in a new era, and it came abruptly on Black Monday, October 28, 1929, when the stock market crashed, and the world cascaded into the Great Depression. This economic calamity triggered ten years of financial misery. Money was no longer something to be used frivolously. It was something that stood between a person and starvation. To make things even worse, World War II followed on the heels of the Depression. Now women didn't have to choose between wealth or good looks in a potential partner, as there was very little money and few able-bodied men available.

Once the war and depression ended, people could get back to living. Or so it would seem. But the unbridled zest for living life to the fullest that was a part of life in the 1920s wasn't the world to which people returned.

In the 1950s, people wanted a return to normalcy by focusing on the family. The American Dream was now a single-family home, a car, and children. This nuclear family lived in the suburbs and consisted of a provider dad, nurturing mom, and two or three children. A poll conducted in 1956 and published in *Life Magazine* listed the attributes of an ideal man according to the typical 1950s woman. The top three characteristics were that he was tall, blue-eyed, and honest. There was no mention of bulging biceps or seething sexuality. Money was ranked number eight and didn't specify anything other than that he held a steady job. Women were looking for stability, not flash.

The book, *The Man in the Gray Flannel Suit,* published in 1955 was symbolic of the middle-class conformity that was required to attain the American Dream. The male in the title role followed strict rules for what it was to be a man. He dressed conservatively and was always careful never to do anything that was considered feminine. There was no fluidity between gender roles during this era. Women were taught to stroke a man's ego and be deferential. In return they would be taken care of by a man who was the ultimate breadwinner. Men outnumbered women in the workplace five to two. Although in the 1950s, women might have had fantasies of being held by handsome blue-eyed actor Paul Neuman, in the real world they would pick a man who could put food on their table. Did this mean that, like Sandy in the movie *Grease*, a woman might want to go to the dance with cute bad boy Danny Zuko, but in the end would marry a solid and responsible man like Ozzie in the 1950s show *Ozzie and Harriet*?

The 1960s and 1970s was the age of counterculture opposing the rigid masculinity and stifling domesticity that guided people's lives in the 1950s. The makeup of the family changed as women rejected mandates of the past that declared that they should know their place, and that place was the home. They wanted more. They no longer told their misbehaving children, "Wait until your father comes home," as they were more than capable of setting their kids straight. The women of these two decades had very different ideas about what they wanted from life. Their new attitude was highlighted in the book, *The Feminine Mystique* by Betty Friedan. The book challenged society's directive that stated to be feminine you couldn't work, get an education, or have a political opinion. It also revealed that many housewives were unhappy despite being financially supported and being married with children.

Once women acknowledged their capabilities and desires, they no longer wanted a man just to find security in their lives. In the 1960s and 1970s, the clean-cut, fatherly male of the '50s was no longer considered attractive. Now, some women were turned on by androgynous rock icons like David Bowie and Mick Jagger. Long hair and pony tales were no longer reserved just for women. Men and women became cultural revolutionaries promoting altruistic values in place of monetary gains, with a segment of the society, the hippies, totally eschewing money. Although most women during these eras didn't subscribe to the sex, drugs, and rock 'n' roll philosophy, they wanted to explore what life had to offer and didn't want to depend on a man to be fulfilled emotionally or financially. This attitude would lead us to believe that women thought that a man's worth depended more on his appearance than his wealth.

In the twenty-first century, the successful yet unfinished fight for women's rights finally caused the pendulum to swing in a direction that dramatically changed a woman's image of the ideal male. The hyper-masculinity of ancient times that created women's total dependence on men for their subsistence was no longer a desired male trait. Instead, women expected to have autonomy over their lives as they assumed leadership roles in the workplace, and their financial independence meant that the modern woman no longer needed a man for financial security. If they wanted a new car or home, they could buy it for themselves.

So, what does this modern woman value in a man? Women have finally attained many of the goals that in the past were thought to be inaccessible. They became more discerning about the qualities that they were searching for in a romantic partner. If appearance was a consideration, a man needed more than a handsome face and buff body to be considered attractive. Instead, a man needed to be intellectually stimulating, have an amusing personality, be culturally knowledgeable, and socially conscious. They also needed to remember that, unlike in the past that, "Money can't buy me love." Or can it?

There are so many examples of young women marrying much older wealthy men that it makes me wonder about the newfound autonomy. Were these modern women really blinded by love, or were they entranced at the thought of having a relationship with their very own King Midas?

Here are a few of these puzzling relationships for you to think about. The media mogul Rupert Murdoch married Jerry Hall when he was eighty-four years old, and she was fifty-nine. Television personality Larry King married a woman in her forties when he was in his seventies. Our last couples deserve a trophy for the greatest age disparity in their relationships. Silvio Berlusconi, the former Italian prime minister, married his wife when he was in his seventies and she was in her twenties. There is a forty-year age gap between George Soros and his wife. And just to spice up the mix we have to mention Woody Allen who had a long-term relationship with his partner's adopted daughter. She was thirty years younger than him.

Maybe these women truly loved these men and didn't notice the gray hair and aging bodies. I'm a little cynical and wonder if these women might have some daddy issues, or if these women had calculated how much time they'd have to wait until they could claim sole ownership of the pot of gold their men had earned. Okay, so maybe I'm a little more than a little cynical about these matchups. How about you?

Nonetheless, if we're to accept the premise that most modern women value a man's appearance over his financial status, then we need to understand why men might hope that the reverse is true. There are always opportunities for a man to increase his wealth. Many men subscribe to the philosophy uttered in the movie *Scarface* by Al Pacino that, "First you get the money, then you get the power, then you get the women." On the other hand, men don't have the vast array of artificial enhancements that women use to enhance their looks. No one is pitching to them the perfect eye makeup or lipstick that will transform them from a somewhat homely man to a handsome one. Thankfully, good looks are subjective and often depend on the eye of the beholder. However, when magazines like *People* announce a yearly sexiest man alive, you can be sure they're not talking about a man's skills or sense of humor. Past winners like George Clooney, Brad Pitt and Chris Evans all meet a certain standard for a man's appearance that most men will never attain.

By the end of 2022, reports indicate that online dating services had over four hundred million active users worldwide. It's very difficult for a man to attract a woman on dating sites like Tinder if they are unattractive. These sites use desirability algorithms that leave no room for criteria such as intelligence, personality, culture, or social consciousness. The algorithms match people of similar appearance to ensure more right-hand swipes (interest in the person). Short bios can contain information on a person's financial status, but that information can easily be embellished, while photos are usually more difficult to falsify. Can this new reality of online dating affect men's impression of whether women value a man's money or looks more?

Now, let's look at the results of our survey, which contradict our earlier premise that a woman's newfound independence and the meat-market ambiance of online dating would elevate appearance to the number one spot of desired characteristics in a woman's attraction to a man.

MEN'S RESPONSES

IMPORTANT MALE ATTRIBUTES	PERCENTAGE
Financial status	46
Appearance	23
Both	11
Don't know	11
Depends on the woman	9

It's interesting to note that in our last chapter 73 percent of our male respondents agreed that they would be comfortable with a woman financially supporting them or earning more than they earned. These men apparently appreciate the value of money. Their ranking of financial status the highest on the survey in this chapter indicates that they attribute this same appreciation to a woman's valuation of a man.

Some of the male respondent's comments noted below are tinged with sadness as they acknowledge this belief and yet their remarks still express the hope that a woman desires more than just money or good looks from a man.

- "Financial status. Sadly, most women today only care about what he can bring to the table financially and nothing else."
- "Yes, woman place more importance on a man's financial status . . . but not just only that . . . especially on honorable, fair and ethical."
- "Both, so many women that I know ignore many wonderful men (and women) because they are not tall or are losing their hair or not making six figures. It makes me sad."
- "Financial status, definitely. My wife has admitted this to me, as has every other woman who I have spoken to about this."

Our women survey respondents really hit the mark in their assumptions that financial status was what men thought women valued most in a relationship, as indicated by the only 5 percent difference in the men's and women's responses.

WOMEN'S RESPONSES

IMPORTANT MALE ATTRIBUTES	PERCENTAGE
Financial status	51
Appearance	20
Both	15
Don't know	15
Depends on the woman	9

Some of our woman respondents, however, seem to resent men when correlating the possession of money with power and control.

- "I think most women should learn to live their lives without men or they will be slaves."
- "I think that immature men believe women to be gold diggers in order to excuse the lack of a relationship/ability to contribute to a relationship."

- "I think that a man who is in the lower financial brackets thinks a woman is initially concerned about appearance and looking for a comfortable financial budget that can support the needs of a family, while women who have been raised in a home where there was no lack of luxury may be more interested in a well-stocked bank book."
- "Tough one. Many women are greedy and want LOADS of money. Others are incredibly vain and want a good-looking guy."
- "I am frequently confused by how much importance guys online seem to think women place on either because if your opening line is 'I'm hot and rich, you should like me' my reaction is 'EW,' but I know people who genuinely don't find that off-putting."

Our female respondent's comments don't do much to negate men's negative perspective that many women are looking for sugar daddies in a relationship.

Movies like *Breakfast at Tiffany's* perpetuate the fantasy of a young woman searching for a rich, older man to marry. Is it possible that men also are looking for sugar mommies? Our next question attempts to identify what attracts a man to a woman. I know what I'm thinking. How about you?

CHAPTER 8

HOT BABE TO UGLY HAG. HOW LOOKS AFFECT THE FICKLE NATURE OF ATTRACTION

How important is a woman's looks in your attraction to her? And does this attraction wane as a woman ages? Perhaps the easiest way to help a man refine his thoughts before he answers this question is to have him envision himself as he was in his early twenties and out with his friends at a crowded singles bar. He and his friends approach a group of women. He doesn't know anything about these women other than what he can see. Two of the women could be models and are wearing very revealing outfits, one is plain looking and dressed conservatively, and one is overweight and homely. He should now ask himself which of these ladies would he try to engage in conversation? Okay, now our man needs to fast forward fifty years and think about the same woman that excited him in the bar. She's obviously changed quite a bit and has white hair, wrinkles and has put on a bit of weight and yet her essence as a person hasn't changed. Does he think that he would still be attracted to the same woman?

Our three friends, Jim, Buddy, and Noah, are no longer in their twenties, and might be a little embarrassed about the basis for their attraction to a woman. They'd probably like to have people think that they're not shallow enough to judge a woman by her looks only, but would that be the truth?

As the friends get ready to again bare their souls, Jim thinks back to his days as a single man in order to recall how important looks were in his attraction to a woman. He has to admit that he would definitely hit on a hot looking woman if he had to pick among a group of strangers. Not only did this appeal to his raging hormones at the time, but it also made his friends jealous when they saw him out with such fantastic eye candy under arm.

Jim tells his friends, "Back then, a girl's personality and intelligence came in second place to her appearance on my dating wish list. I also think that I should clarify what I mean by her appearance. A girl could be well dressed and nice looking but not make the cut. My definition of a woman's desirable appearance had to do with her sensuality. She had to wear sexy clothes, move, and talk seductively and might even physically be described as a little quirky looking. I guess you might say that I wouldn't be impressed if I met the most beautiful woman in the world if she lacked sex appeal. My views as a married man haven't changed much. I'll boast that I hit the jackpot when I met my wife Claire, because she was physically beautiful as well as sexy. I can't see my attraction to her ever fading. Even if her beauty dims, her sensuality will remain because it's a part of her essence. However, I'm not foolish enough to think that all men feel like I do. I have friends who trade in their wives when they turn forty for new trophy wives. Not only are they unable to look beneath the surface in a partner, but they also think that their masculinity is enhanced when they have a young, glamorous wife."

Buddy interrupts. "Hey guys, I thought that we were going to be totally honest. We're talking about flesh-and-blood women, not essences like a perfume scent. Jim is trying to sugarcoat what he's really saying. Men are attracted to women who act, dress, look, and talk sexy. It doesn't matter if they're plain looking, glamorous, talkative, quiet, stupid, or smart, as long as they radiate sexuality. Just like the Bible says a man needs to help a woman fulfill her role in life to be fruitful and multiply. For me to successfully perform my part in that mandate, I need a woman to fulfill my sexual fantasies. The older I get the more help I need. I don't want a virginal, shy woman. I've been asked if I get bored with a woman who is all looks and no brains. I always respond that's why television was created. I'm not less attracted to a woman when she gets older as long as she continues to satisfy my sexual needs." Buddy looks at prim and proper Noah to gauge his reaction.

Surprisingly, Noah is nodding in agreement with Buddy. Noah explains to his friends, "Before I met Jane, I had a difficult time resisting the allure of my female students. I definitely wasn't attracted to them because of their intellects or personalities. It was pure lust, and that lust was reserved for the most sensuous looking girls. However, let me qualify my response by saying that although I liked a provocative looking woman, I got turned off by any behavior that hinted of a licentious nature. I liked to think that these girls were unaware that their appearance enticed men. It was up to me to awaken their hidden charms. I must admit that I felt an enormous amount of power in my role as love-teacher to a woman. As a woman ages and becomes wiser in the ways of the world, I think that she no longer sees a man as a masterful guru. It's this diminished look of adoration that's reflected in her eyes that lessens my attraction to her. Like Buddy, I don't really care if a woman is traditionally beautiful. It's more important to me that she's in touch with her own passions, as long as she acknowledges my dominant role in the relationship."

Apparently, our three men agree that a woman's looks are a very important factor in their attraction to her. However, none of our men define looks to mean a pretty face. The one word that sums up their description of what female looks attract a man is the word *sexy*. Jim and Buddy think a woman can be a hot mama at any age, so their attraction to a woman doesn't change because she gets older. Noah is more into the me "Tarzan, you Jane" scenario, and in his mind an older woman can't become a Jane. The Bible had a lot to say about the importance of a woman's appearance in a man's attraction to her. However, despite the exhortation that women should exude purity because her beauty is connected to her moral character, many biblical stories reek of sexual improprieties.

YESTERDAY

It's difficult to know where to begin when giving examples of the importance of a woman's looks in biblical relationships as there are so many interesting illustrations to cite. No matter where I start it seems that very few couples in biblical times took seriously the instructions to remain pure. It's true that some relationships were based on the fact that the family—not the couple—chose their mates for betrothal and therefore attraction wasn't important. However, let's have some fun and focus on the juicier biblical stories.

Bathsheba was bathing when David saw her from his palace roof. His lust for her was so great that it only took one glimpse of her beauty for him to know that he had to have her at any cost. This was unfortunate for Bathsheba's husband, as the cost to him was his life. After seeing Bathsheba, David immediately sent his servants to find her. He slept with her, and she became pregnant. Meanwhile David sent her poor husband to the frontline of a fierce battle where he was killed. Obviously, David wasn't driven to distraction by Bathsheba's wit or brains as he decided to bed her before he ever spoke to her. He was captivated by her beauty. It's clear that he paid no attention to the dictate, "Do not lust in your heart after her beauty or let her captivate you with her eyes" (Proverbs 6:25). David remained married to Bathsheba until he died. He could have easily replaced her with a younger woman if he no longer found her desirable, and yet her age didn't seem to matter to him.

The Israeli Queen Jezebel was the epitome of a woman who proudly declared her sexual autonomy and used her seductive powers to lead men into evil. To this day her name is associated with morally unrestrained women. Again, it was not her brain that was the most important element of her power over men, although she was a master at manipulating men to fulfill her desires. She combined her dominant personality with her sexual promiscuity to attract men, even attempting to seduce Jehu, the man charged with murdering her.

The Bible is notoriously lax in its descriptions of a person's physical appearance, but in Jezebel's case it paints a vivid picture of her splendor. She was always portrayed with her face fully made up and wearing elaborate wigs. She even went so far as to carefully paint her eyes as she went to her death. It's possible that under all that makeup Jezebel was actually homely, but it didn't matter as her main attraction to men was her sexuality. Jezebel's seductiveness persevered as she got older, and when she died at the age of fifty-nine she was still kicking up her heels.

The story of Abraham and Sarah falls more in line with the traditional biblical construct of what constituted a relationship. The wife was totally obedient to her husband even if that meant that the husband would lend his female partner to other men to save his own life. The accounts of their relationship show that they both believed that their bond was preordained. This might have been the case, however all descriptions of Sarah note that she was incredibly beautiful and that this beauty was probably the reason why Abraham and other men were so attracted to her. Her beauty never faded. But Sarah found out when she was sixty-five years of age that her beauty could be dangerous.

As the narrative goes, the pharaoh wanted Sarah but knew it would bring the wrath of the gods if he took a married woman away from her husband. Abraham didn't think it betrayed his love for Sarah when he asked her to tell the Pharoah that she was his sister and not his wife. Now, the pharaoh could feel comfortable bedding Sarah without fear of retribution, and in addition, Abraham profited from their union. Meanwhile, Sarah went to live with the pharaoh until he realized that he had been fooled. He then sent Sarah back to Abraham. Sarah was now ninety years old and still so beautiful that King Abimelech of Gerar kidnapped her from Abraham. Abraham again asked her to protect him by saying she was his sister, not his wife, until, once again, his trick was uncovered. Sarah was very spiritual, and the word seductress was the last thing you would use to describe her. She was simply ravishingly beautiful, and this attracted men to her like a bee is attracted to a flower's nectar. Abraham obviously enjoyed Sarah's beauty not only for his own pleasure, but also as a tool to use as a form of barter.

THE IMAGES OF partially nude women of ancient Greece would make someone think that sexual attraction was the main focus that drew a man to a woman during that time. However, the reason that women bared their breasts was because, back then, breasts weren't a taboo body part that had to be covered. A woman's primary role in society was to be a breeder, and her breasts were simply an organ to feed her child. Both married and single women wore a veil over their faces when they appeared in public or before unrelated males. What was it then that attracted a man in ancient Greece to a woman if they weren't preoccupied with a woman's breasts and couldn't see their face? Much of the literature indicates that a woman's long hair and voice were a magnetic source of attraction to men in ancient Greece. An older woman could still attract a man with a lovely voice and long hair. Oh, and let's not forget that a unibrow was considered the height of beauty, and everyone could grow one of those. It's amazing the types of criteria people use to decide on their choice of a partner.

Almost everyone recognizes the name Cleopatra and yet it's rarely mentioned that she was an outstanding representative of women's equality. The status of women in Ancient Egypt was opposite to that of women in ancient Greece. Although movies would have us believe that it was Cleopatra's amazing beauty that mesmerized men, many accounts describe her as quirky looking. Cleopatra and the women in Ancient Egypt weren't viewed as the chattel of men. They didn't need the supervision or approval of a man in order to pursue a course of action. They could marry anyone they chose, and in most divorces the woman got the children and the home. Virginity was still prized, but if a woman was sexually experienced before marriage she was not condemned. They had the same legal rights and status as men. Women like Nefertiti and Cleopatra could even rule their country. How did this influence the basis for a man's attraction to a woman during this era?

Men and women of Ancient Egypt interacted with each other socially so they could actually talk instead of relying on mating arrangements made and supervised by their families. Both men and women paid a lot of attention to their appearances using elaborate jewelry, makeup, wigs, and clothing to enhance their attributes. Sex was an important act of creation and as normal as eating or sleeping. This perspective made it easy for a man to get to third base with a woman. However, the ordinariness of sexuality let a man see beyond *sexy* when looking for a mate. Men in Ancient Egypt could consider a woman attractive because of her mind, strength, and personality. Yet, a woman's physical beauty could still turn a man's head as demonstrated in the relationship of Ramses the Great and Nefertari. Ramses words about Nefertari says it all, "My love is unique . . . no one can rival her, for she is the most beautiful woman alive. Just by passing, she has stolen away my heart."

On the other hand, older women didn't fare too well in Ancient Egypt. The ancient Egyptians believed that you would look the same in the afterlife as you did while you were alive. Apparently, no one wanted to look the way they did when they were older, as their art always depicted women as young. It was believed that young women were at the peak of their beauty and energy. Older women no longer incited passion in men.

I think by now we can agree that different eras had different beauty standards and what in the past was a social norm could become taboo in the present day. As we've discovered, in the past it might have been common for a man to see a woman walking down the street bare breasted. However, it would be a different story today. At the very least, it would probably be the cause of major car crashes as male drivers eagerly tried to catch a glimpse of a topless woman. The sexualization of a woman's breast may be the reason that many men are so intrigued by the sight of it and consider it a major factor in gauging a woman's attractiveness. What is it that they say about the allure of the forbidden? In Ancient Egypt, a woman's beauty consisted of many factors, and men were enthralled by this beauty more than a woman's physical sexuality. Was this true in later eras?

When we think of the Victorian era, images of repressed, strait-laced ladies come to mind. Supposedly, the Victorians were so prudish that they even covered up table legs in cloths so men wouldn't be tempted by a peek at a woman's ankles. The reality of sexual activity in Victorian society, however, was sometimes quite different from those depicted in stories. Venereal disease was rampant. Pornography was a big business. By 1834, fifty-seven illegal porn shops were operating on Holywell Street in London, and both men and women could be seen window shopping outside these stores (metro.co.uk).

All of this preoccupation with sex in the Victorian era would seem to indicate that men would be attracted to women based on their sexual appeal, but the opposite would probably fit their image of what they wanted in a woman as their partner. It was important that a woman be a *lady*, and this didn't depend on wealth. The most important characteristics for a woman to possess was morality, respectability, and social conduct. She was thought of as physically delicate and needed to maintain her modesty at all costs. Most importantly, a woman had to hide sexual urges. If a woman possessed all of the above qualities she would be guaranteed to attract a man. Her sexuality was not a part of the equation.

Makeup was for loose woman, and therefore a Victorian women's skin had to be flawless. Victorian women spent hours layering their faces with lead masks to keep their youthful glow. Men were advised to look at a perspective mate carefully as the only thing that they could see before marriage was what was visible above the neckline of clothing. Much of a man's attraction to a woman stemmed from her gentle nature and proficiency in her role as the family's caretaker.

As a woman aged, she was no longer considered a fragile flower and was now able to participate in more public roles in society. But to men, these new freedoms were viewed as a woman's rejection of her femininity and, therefore, diminished her desirability. The Victorian age was not a welcoming place for older women.

It was widely accepted in Victorian times that melancholia was a condition that afflicted many women, and the art of the time displayed disturbing images of women under stressful circumstances. The famous painting *Ophelia*, John Everette Millais portrays a woman who purposely lets herself drown after the death of her father. It's interesting to note that even in death, the painting depicts the woman as beautiful. Elizabeth Siddal was the model for this painting, and yet her beauty contradicted the norm of female beauty that existed during this time. She was slim and had red hair. These were two characteristics that were considered ugly by most people living then however, in the eyes of the pre-Raphaelite artists Millais, Walter Deverell, and Dante Rossette, Siddal exemplified supreme beauty. Deverell called her "stupendously beautiful," while Rossette's drawings of her numbered into the thousands. She became Dante's muse, and he married her toward the end of her life when the arsenic compound that she used to maintain her wonderful complexion finally killed her. Dante was also a poet. He had Siddal exhumed to retrieve the book of poems that he had buried with her. A myth still exists that when her tomb was opened, her beauty was still intact, and her glorious red hair had continued growing to fan out around her head. These artists couldn't resist the pull of a woman's beauty and believed that beauty prevailed even after death.

TODAY

World War I and the Spanish flu were responsible for millions of deaths. Once these disasters were in the past people could finally start living again, and boy did they live. The 1920s was a time of major social upheavals in which most of the moral constraints of past decades were discarded. When once the sole reason for finding a love interest was to marry and have a family, this search now became a means for casual social entertainment. Women wanted to enjoy what life had to offer, and this meant no longer being under the control of a man.

The flapper epitomized this new era of frenzied fun in which women could go to clubs by themselves, ask men out on dates, and hold important jobs outside the home. Their dresses and hair were short, and their figures were the opposite of the Victorian standard of exaggerated clinched waists and feminine curves. If compared to anything, it could be said that a boyish figure was prized, and the flapper would do anything to flaunt conventional norms of the past, even if it meant binding their breasts. Their appearance and behavior underscored their equality with men.

Although this equality still wasn't attainable in every aspect of society, there were new attitudes in conventional institutions such as marriage. Companionship was now considered an important factor in marriage. Some men felt threatened by a no longer submissive type of woman. On the other hand, men also were excited by the atmosphere created by this *new woman* who danced, smoked, drank alcohol, and attended *petting parties*. A woman's beauty was seen as more than her physical attributes. It was now based on a fire burning inside her that drew in every man she met. Her independence, vitality and zest for living was entrancing. Zelda Fitzgerald, wife of F. Scott Fitzgerald, personified the flapper, contradicting the fallacy that flappers were ditsy. She was a published writer, trained dancer, and artist. She was idolized by her husband because of all of her qualities and freedoms.

Men in the 1920s didn't have to choose a woman based on beauty, sex appeal or intelligence, as the flapper could possess all of these traits. Perhaps it could be said that the most important thing in a man's attraction to a woman in the 1920s was her exuberance for living. It's not possible to discover if this attraction would have waned as a woman got older because this groundbreaking time of change abruptly came to an end with the depression of 1929. The next few decades halted the progress of many of the freedoms won for women in the 1920s. Just like in ancient times, a woman's submissiveness was again prized in the 1940s and 1950s. A man was head of the home, and his word was law in his family. And then it was the 1960s and the era of free love had begun.

In the 1960s, a man's attraction to a woman was based on a very simple concept. If a woman was willing to have sexual relations with a man, then they were attractive, and female hippies were always ready to make love. Male and female hippies reviled anything that supported materialism and repression and instead wanted anything that would promote their enlightenment. They freely used hallucinogenic drugs like LSD to expand their consciousness and add excitement to their sexual encounters. The Summer of Love and Woodstock were Hippie events where the mantra of "Make love, not war," was loudly declared.

The Vietnam War had begun in 1955, and by the 1960s people had to take sides as protestors or supporters of the war. Women were giving out sexual favors to men who rejected military service. Even famous woman like Joan Baez supported this action by appearing in photos titled, *Girls say yes to boys who say no*. This generation rejected their parent's lifestyle and followed Timothy Leary's directives to "Turn on, tune in, and drop out."

Although hippies were mostly young, older women would be accepted as a man's love interest if she subscribed to the open sexual philosophy of these flower children. Because of human nature, it's probably true to say that hippies were more attracted to a pretty girl than a homely one. However, the combination of free love and drugs blurred the line defining whether looks or sex was the most important factor in a man's attraction to a woman in the hippie era. Hippies started a counterculture that was the beginning of the gender revolution and whose influence would affect many later generations.

The hippie influence is still felt today. Many people today live together without being married, use pot legally, accept gender fluidity, gay marriage, show concern about the environment, accept tattoos as a mainstream, and are open to the use of nudity and profanity in the media. By the mid-1970s the hippie movement had faded away as one of the reasons for its existence, the Vietnam War, had ended and many hippies succumbed to the lure of making money in a normal job. These ex-hippies became known as yuppies (young urban professionals) and the teeter-totter of what constituted physical attraction between men and women again changed.

—

IN THE LATER years of the twentieth century women had attained many of the rights that they had been denied in earlier decades. Women were in control of their own identities, and their job opportunities were no longer restricted to the nursing, secretarial, and teaching professions. Women took to the gym in record numbers, and the ideal figure was embodied in the hardbody of actresses like Jane Fonda. Women were independent and weren't seduced by men. Everything that they did was by choice. Women projected a corporate image and wanted a mature man to help them achieve their goals. It was not only women who redefined their roles in society. Men willingly—or begrudgingly—had to assume many of the responsibilities of family life that once were the exclusive province of their wives. Did these new role parameters affect a man's attraction to a woman?

By the beginning of this century, thanks to the wonders of modern cosmetic enhancements, a woman's physical appearance could be altered so much that what a man saw when he gazed at a woman one day could be drastically different from what he saw in the future. On April 15, 2002, the FDA approved Botox as a cosmetic treatment to remove lines and wrinkles, and now, with the prick of a needle, women could easily change the face that they presented to the world and hold back the ravages of time. Female attractiveness was attainable for every woman.

However, the bigger question in a male-female relationship in modern times was whether the man and woman were in sync with their new gender roles. Was the woman still looking for her knight in shining armor, and could a man come second in importance to a woman's job? Good looks will probably always count in attraction, but it may not be the most important thing in what constitutes a woman's appeal to a man.

Let's think again about the relationship of Bill and Hillary Clinton. To most observers, Hillary wasn't the sexiest or most beautiful woman when Bill married her in 1975, but he might have sensed that her intelligence and ambition would be an asset to him in the future. During the 1980s and 1990s they created a political powerhouse, and although Bill may have had eyes for other women, he knew that Hillary possessed something that couldn't be seen with the naked eye. Because the root of Bill's attraction to Hillary wasn't based on looks, an attribute that might not have long-term permanence, it's unlikely that this attraction would fade as she aged.

The twenty-first century man isn't shy about admitting that he has feelings and that those feelings can be hurt. Although men of this period appreciate beauty, they are also sensitive to any intimation of harassment that might come from paying too much attention to a woman's looks. These men haven't been repressed sexually as men of the past, so they don't spend every minute fantasizing about a woman's breasts. They were probably raised by a mother who emphasized that men and women deserved equal rights, and this has led him to respect a woman's search for autonomy, or at the very least, he knows to pretend that he does. It seems that we can say definitively for the modern man, a woman's looks are not the most important thing in his attraction to her, whether she is a young girl or an older woman. Much of what can be researched about relationships during this century indicates that this observation is correct.

Now, let's check on the results of our survey to learn if our male respondents agree with our observations on female attractiveness.

MEN'S RESPONSES

IMPORTANCE OF LOOKS	PERCENTAGE
Looks are the most important	66
Looks are not the most important	21
Not sure about the importance	8
Looks depend on different factors/genetics	5
DOES ATTRACTION WANE WITH AGE	**PERCENTAGE**
Attraction wanes with age	44
Attraction doesn't wane with age	34
Not sure if attraction wanes with age	15
Attraction waning with age depends on different factors/genetics	7

It's not surprising that men would say that looks are the most important criterion in their attraction to a woman as men respond to visual stimulation. It is a bit surprising, however, that almost a quarter of the responses indicated that a woman's looks are not the most important thing in a man's attraction to her. The responses are almost equally divided on the question of attraction waning with age. Some of our male respondents dug deep into their feelings before they answered our question, as evidenced by some of the following comments:

- "Very important, yes it wanes but so does the importance. This question strongly depends on the time in a person's life that the question was asked, are they looking for a strong family with kids or someone to be their best friend in their twilight years, the answer will vary."
- "Again, this depends upon the woman, but attraction is the main starting factor for me. I'm not going to date someone who

is not attractive to me. Though, chemistry will quickly become the main reason whether I will stay with someone."

- "A woman's physical appearance is very important, and yes, this attraction wanes as a woman ages. This is biologically factual. A younger female is more attractive to a male mate because a man is a visual animal; her physical characteristics appeal to him from a sexual procreative aspect. As a woman ages, this decreases, thereby ensuring the male mate only focuses on young mates to ensure his progeny may survive and guarantee the survival of his tribe/race/species. This is why older women are not seized by males during raids, attacks etc. The reason why relationships last to old age in our society today is due to emotional connection, not physical attraction."

Whew, our last respondent's comment might cause some women to turn against science, at least as to how it's interpreted by this respondent. A few of our male respondents suggested specific specifications that constituted good looks in a woman.

- "Depends, if she still smiles."
- "The most physically attractive woman may have an ugly personality."
- "As she ages, she looks the same as you remember."
- "Meh, I'm more concerned about her being healthy in general . . . an obese BMI//failure to maintain any kind of fitness//etc. is a huge turn-off."
- "All women under eighty years of age look good to me."

The comment of our last male respondent should give hope to all older ladies, unless you're over eighty and then according to his inference, you're probably invisible to him.

Our female respondents weren't charitable in their judgments of men regarding the basis of their attraction to women.

WOMEN'S RESPONSES

IMPORTANCE OF LOOKS	PERCENTAGE
Looks are the most important	74
Looks are not the most important	5
Not sure about the importance	11
Looks depend on different factors/genetics	10
DOES ATTRACTION WANE WITH AGE	**PERCENTAGE**
Attraction wanes with age	54
Attraction doesn't wane	25
Not sure if attraction wanes	11
Attraction waning with age depends on different factors/genetics	10

Clearly, the female responses indicate, at least in part, a jaded view of a man's attraction to a woman. Apparently, the personal experiences these women have had with men have led them to believe that a man's desire for a woman is predicated almost solely on the woman's looks. Here are a few of those comments.

- "Very important and I do believe attraction wanes. Most famous or rich men go for beautiful women way younger, so if the average male had the option I'm sure he'd pick youth over character."
- "Very important, yes it wanes: most men are shallow."
- "Very important, yes, men are pigs."
- "Women's looks matter to men a lot of the time because they are arrogant pigs."
- "VERY. Yes. Some men can be just as superficial as women and don't want to be seen out with their 'mother.'"

- "Very important as males are more visual. He attraction does wane explaining the high incidence of infidelity, frequently starting when his partner is pregnant.'
- "All important; yes, even when they're old and pot-bellied they wish they had eye candy."

Finally, our last female respondent's comment noted below indicates that she would probably be a good match with our male respondent who cited science for his reasoning.

- "Very important due to trying to find a mate to bear children with. If you look at it from an evolutionary perspective, it does wane over time especially when she can't bear children anymore."

I guess that this last comment can be interpreted to mean that if a woman is sterile she has no hopes of attracting a man.

Ultimately, it seems that the consensus of both male and female survey respondents is that looks are the most important factor in a man's attraction to a woman. However, many more women than male respondents believed that a man's attraction to a woman diminishes as she ages.

Nonetheless we have to remember that not everyone's definition of good looks is the same. In Japan, from the twelfth through nineteenth centuries, the symbol of beauty in a woman was black teeth—*Ohaguro*. Japanese woman also had dental work done—*Yaeba*—to create a crooked smile because it was believed this practice would make a woman less perfect and therefore more approachable to a man. And let's not forget the prominent stomachs of the Renaissance women or the mustached women of nineteenth century Iran. If we think about this lack of uniformity in classifying beauty throughout the ages, then we come to the realization that someone's attraction is often influenced by societal norms.

Does the acknowledgment that the most important thing in a

man's attraction to a woman is her good looks mean that men can only be friends with physically homely women? Or, regardless of whether a woman is or isn't good looking, is there some undercurrent of sexual tension that always exists between men and women that make being *just* friends impossible. That's something that we'll learn more about in our next chapter.

CHAPTER 9

THE FRIEND ZONE: WHERE A MAN'S DREAMS GO TO DIE

Some of the female respondent's comments might lead us to believe that men are wild-eyed, lustful beasts who at the sight of a woman are unable to control their urges to mate. An alternative way of considering whether men and women can be *just* friends is to reflect on some of the characteristics that most people associate with good relationships. It's usually agreed that liking your partner, sharing common interests, and enjoying time with one another is essential. These attributes also gird the foundation of friendship. Therefore, some would argue that what starts as friendship will invariably evolve into something else. On the other hand, I'm sure that many of you reading this can think of a friendship you've had with someone of the opposite sex that never went beyond a plutonic bonding. Jim, Buddy, and Noah will surely have insightful thoughts on this question.

Jim is glad that this question has come up when only the guys are around as he might be nervous that his wife wouldn't like his answer. Many of his coworkers are women. Jim thinks that some of them have decided to push the envelope and interpret their fight against gender bias to mean not just attaining fair pay and equal employment opportunities but also having the freedom to be as sexually promiscuous as some men. Women who view a man's wedding ring as an intriguing challenge to their sexual autonomy have become sexual predators. Jim says he has never been tempted to cheat on his wife, but he admits that he has eyes in his head and can't help but look at a woman if she is attractive. However, he makes sure that a woman never sees his roaming eyes for fear that she might consider his glare an invitation to play around. Because of this, Jim finds the idea of becoming friends with a female officemate preposterous.

Jim frequently has to stay late in the office to finish putting together business deals, and many times his working partner is a sexually liberated woman. As he tells Buddy and Noah, "I make sure that our bodies never touch, and every so often, I mention what a beautiful wife I have. But this comment about my wife is the only personal reference that I ever make. I do everything that I can to make it clear that I don't have personal relationships with people in my office. It's sad that I have to do this because there are some nice people at work who seem to want to establish a friendship with me, and yet I have to stick with my no-friends-in-the-office policy. It must sound like I'm extremely conceited to think that the women in my office are just waiting to hit on me. In addition, I'm sure that my hesitancy to have female friends could imply that I'm so sex crazed that I can't control myself around a woman. But I'd rather sound narcissistic or like a sex maniac than take a chance on doing anything that would damage my relationship with my wife. I would still say no to a friendship with a woman even if I could guarantee that she clearly had no designs on me. To me, friendship means being yourself with someone and not having to watch your words or actions. I couldn't have those feelings with any woman except my wife or my male buddies."

Buddy decides to chime in. "I love women, but not for the same reasons that I love my friends. I know that sounds confusing until I explain that I only have guy friends. One thing that Jim didn't mention is that friends have to have things in common. I suppose that I could find a woman who likes to sit around in her underwear and watch sports on television while getting a beer buzz or be satisfied eating fast food seven nights a week. However, even then I'd probably be thinking about what she looks like minus her underwear or worrying that all that fast food will take a toll on her figure. These things would never enter my mind if I were with my buddies. Unlike Jim, I'm proud of my masculinity and my thoughts about the appropriate relationship between a man and a woman underscore the natural order of things."

Buddy continues. "Men and women are meant to be sexually attracted to each other in order to fulfill their role in procreation. When I meet a woman, I don't envision us together at a football game unless it means we'll also be with each other later that night when I'll score my own touchdown. Jim is worried that some people might think he can't control himself around women. The only time a man should worry about something like that is if he tricks a woman into thinking that he only wants to be her friend so he can get close to her, or if he tries to force himself on her. I'm honest with women, whether they are my coworkers or women that I meet socially. I make it clear that when I'm at my job I'm there to work, not make friends. When I meet women socially, unless they're married, my behavior immediately lets them know that I'm coming on to them as a potential romantic connection. But let me backtrack a bit. I always believe in being totally transparent. I said that I only have guy friends, with the exception of my female family members. I'm not an animal. Even if I can appreciate their beauty, I would never allow myself to entertain any lewd thoughts about them."

Noah is stunned by how black and white Buddy and Jim's perspective are on the subject of male-female friendships. He can't imagine not having women friends. He tells Jim and Buddy that, "Women and men experience life in different ways. The most exhilarating thing about being friends with a woman is hearing their viewpoint on things that can provide me with knowledge I'd otherwise never be able to obtain. I'm not willing to give up this intellectual exchange with someone just because I might fleetingly have sexual thoughts about them. Thoughts don't have to translate into action. It's true that in the past I've had to struggle with self-control in dealing with attractive female students, but that issue is different from what we're talking about now. My interest in those students was ignited because of sexual tension. On the other hand, my female friends and

I are stimulated by intellectual pursuits. My girlfriend, Jane, approves of my friendships because she knows that I'm not looking for sexual satisfaction with these female friends."

It sounds like Jim doesn't want to have anything to do with having friends with benefits, while Buddy, however, wants to cut to the chase and go right for the benefits. If Noah is telling the truth, he is able to have female friends because he has learned how to compartmentalize his relationships with women.

We're all familiar with stories of famous love affairs. There are numerous movies and books narrating these often tempestuous and dramatic relationships. However, in comparison, platonic friendships between men and women are rarely considered interesting enough to be chronicled. Nonetheless, there are some accounts of relationships that illustrate the possibility of a man and woman being plutonic platonic friends. Here are a few:

YESTERDAY

The Bible has many proverbs referencing friendship such as, "One who has unreliable friends soon come to ruin, but there is a friend who sticks closer than a brother" (Proverbs 18:24). Unfortunately, for our purposes, most of these friendships in biblical times were between same-gender people. It's difficult to find examples of male-female friendships in ancient literature. Maybe men and women back then were just too hot-blooded to keep their hands off each other.

In 700 BC Homer wrote the *Odyssey*. The story of Odysseus and Nausicaa underscores the futility of a man and a woman being just friends. Nausicaa helps Odysseus find shelter after he is shipwrecked. He becomes a guest in her family's home and over time becomes enamored of her. Nausicaa was willing to help out a friend in need, but just because she was kind to Odysseus didn't mean that she wanted a romantic relationship with him, as she ultimately marries another man. It's said that Homer's description of their relationship is the first example of unrequited love. Nausicaa thought Odysseus was her friend, but he wanted more than friendship from her.

Another instance of friendship between a man and a woman occurred during 51-59 AD. This friendship was between the Apostle Paul and a woman named Phoebe. She was a deacon of the church at Cenchreae and held in such high esteem by Paul that he introduced her as his emissary to the church in Rome. In addition, his great trust in her was demonstrated when he had her deliver his letters to the Romans. This was an honor, as it was not common during this time for a woman to be trusted with such a task. It's conceivable that Buddy was correct about the importance of friends having things in common. Following this train of thought, we can understand how Paul and Phoebe became such good friends. They shared the same spiritual goal and dedication to their God. There was never any intimation of impropriety between them, just a real friendship.

Philosophers such as Aristotle describe friendship as reciprocated goodwill. Aristotle also said that there are several forms of friendship, and that true friendship is when friends love each other for their own sake and wish good things for each other. However, he states that this kind of friendship can only happen between "good people similar in virtue." This might indicate that Aristotle believed in the possibility of male-female friendships, but the truth is the opposite. In his *History of Animals* IX he states that men are more virtuous than women and that women are feeble of mind. Therefore, women could never meet the primary criteria for friendship with men as he believed that they were not similar in virtue. It would have been more accurate to substitute the word *men* for *people* in Aristotle's description of true friendship.

Heterosexual friendships weren't considered truly possible until the Renaissance. However, even then, suspicion still existed around the motivations underlying the friendship between a man and woman. This skepticism was evidenced at the end of the Renaissance in the friendship of Angela Mellini and Giovanni Battista Ruggieri.

Angela was a seamstress in Bologna in the 1690s. One day she walked into her church to tell her parish priest, Giovanni Battista

Ruggieri, about the strange visions that she had been having. Mellini and Ruggieri soon realized that they wanted a reciprocal friendship. She would be his penitent, and he would become her confessor. They got along so well that Giovanni Ruggieri started confiding in her some of his own faults and before too long they were switching roles of confessor and penitent. Not everyone approved of this male-female friendship and before too long they were reported to the Inquisition. Mellini's and Ruggieri's friendship was considered a threat to male clerical authority and their friendship resulted in Ruggieri being exiled.

In the nineteenth century, strict Victorian social norms hampered the development of male-female friendships. Men and women were discouraged from having contact unless that contact was to initiate a relationship leading to marriage.

To avoid any hint of scandal, men and women who wanted to remain friends developed excellent letter-writing skills, as this form of communication was thought appropriate for both genders. However, even this form of communication had guidelines. The quality and color of the paper, pens, and handwriting all had to meet certain standards. However, the postal service during this century was very different from the one we are all familiar with today. The contents of a person's letter were never private. Letters were read by the carrier, and it was common for the recipient to read them to a crowd. There could be no suggestion of any type of intimacy or romantic relationship in the writer's choice of words. The reality was that men and women were still mostly friends with people of their own gender as they bonded over a mutuality of interest in the social and political affairs of society. It's probable that some men and women of the Victorian era flaunted conventions regarding friendship with the opposite sex, but research indicates that these friendships were rarely in the public eye. However, there are a few recorded friendships that straddled the nineteenth and twentieth centuries between famous people such as the inventor Alexander

Graham Bell and Helen Keller, and human rights activists Susan B. Anthony and Frederick Douglas.

Bell met Keller when she was six years old. At the age of eighteen months, she contracted a disease that left her deaf and blind. At that time, people with such disabilities were institutionalized, but Bell spoke out against institutionalizing her. He stood by her and supported her both emotionally and financially. He even learned to use a braille typewriter so he could directly communicate with her. Bell's mother was almost completely deaf. Perhaps this contributed to his belief that he had a lifelong calling to help the deaf community. Among many other kindnesses to Keller, he acted as her personal guide when he took her to the World's Columbia Exposition in Chicago to learn about modern science and technology. He also helped her feel the power of water when he took her to Niagara Falls where he put her hand on a windowpane so that she would be able to feel the water's power, even though she couldn't see or hear it. Bell's sometimes extraordinary efforts to help Keller might have appeared to make their friendship one-sided. But there was nothing one-sided about their friendship as demonstrated by Bell's words about the tremendous satisfaction that he got from his work with the deaf, calling it more pleasing "than even my recognition of my work with the telephone." Both Bell and Keller had a true reciprocity of friendship.

The friendship between Susan B. Anthony and Frederick Douglas challenged gender and racial societal boundaries that existed during the nineteenth century. Anthony was a White woman and Douglas was a man born into slavery. Their friendship existed at a time when interracial relationships of any kind were considered taboo. However, this didn't stop their commitment to align themselves together in the fight against slavery and to fight for women's suffrage and civil rights. More than a few disapproving voices could be heard from members of both the Black and White communities. This backlash caused the White suffragists to back off from any association with Anthony or Douglas, while Black activists also withdrew from the couple because they believed that Anthony prioritized the importance of White women's rights over Black women. Nonetheless, Anthony and Douglas's friendship lasted over forty-five years with no hint of sexual impropriety.

TODAY

By the early twentieth century, women flooded the workplace and institutions of learning. Men and women would now work and learn shoulder to shoulder and being just friends with one another would become more commonplace. By the 1960s, the cry for equality between men and women meant that friendship between genders was no longer something that made people question motives, or at least not openly. There would always be speculation about whether male-female friendships could really exist without having sex. If they were alive today, two famous Hollywood stars would answer that question with a resounding yes.

Rock Hudson and Elizabeth Taylor were best friends for more than thirty years. They traveled and went to award ceremonies together. When Hudson was dying, Taylor snuck into the hospital to see him. This sounds like a passionate love story—and it was—but it was a passionate love for a friend, not a lover. Hudson was a homosexual.

Such everlasting friendships didn't only occur in Hollywood. A friendship that many people would consider unlikely lasted for many years among two United States Supreme Court judges. Ruth Bader Ginsberg and Antonin Scalia met in the 1980s when they both were serving together in the United States Court of Appeals, DC Circuit. They continued to work together for forty years, although they were ideological foes. Their friendship started because of their mutual devotion to the Constitution, and it continued to grow until the death of Scalia. They both grew up in New York, loved the opera, and they and their families spent every New Year's Eve together. Their mutual respect endured even when faced with heated disagreements over Supreme Court cases. When asked about his friendship with

Ginsberg, Scalia responded, "What's not to like? Except her views on the law." There was never a question of whether any romance existed between the two justices. Scalia was a hunter. He would bring fresh game for New Year's Eve dinner, and Martin Ginsberg, Ruth's husband, would make a fabulous meal with it for them to share.

PERHAPS IT IS easier for a man and woman to be just friends if one of them is not heterosexual. A great example of this is Lady Gaga and Elton John. Not only is Gaga friends with John, but she also is a godmother to his two sons. Just like the friendship between Ginsberg and Scalia, having a common interest seems to be essential to a lasting friendship.

Gaga and John first met when they performed together at the Grammy Awards and realized that their love of music and flamboyant taste in fashion made them kindred spirits. Afterward, they continued to work together and solidified their friendship. Although John is much older than Gaga, he said that he admired everything about her and that she would be a great role model for his sons. Gaga has called him her mentor. One might again wonder, just like in the friendship of Hudson and Taylor, if a lack of sexual tension made their friendship so strong.

Apparently, research studies are on the fence about whether men and women can be just friends. A study done at Pennsylvania State University in the year 2000 revealed that of 315 college students, approximately half of them had crossed the line and had sex with their friends. In 2012, another study at the University of Wisconsin queried 107 people between the ages of eighteen and fifty-five to discover the pros and cons of same-sex friendships. More men than women in both groups admitted to feeling an attraction to their female friends. Some of these men hopefully anticipated the friendship turning romantic.

Younger women and both genders in the older age group

who participated in the Wisconsin study disclosed that the sexual attraction that they felt toward their male friends increased if they were less satisfied with their romantic partners. That shoulder to cry on could easily morph into a lingering caress and then a not-so-innocent kiss. Many of the participants in both of the studies stated that their friendships started with attraction to the other person and then became platonic. There was no indication whether this was a case of unrequited love or mutual disinterest. Whatever the actual motivation for a same-gender friendship, it's without a doubt that the answer to whether same-gender friendships are possible is complicated. The studies from Pennsylvania State University and the University of Wisconsin have given us some insight into this topic, however, they are more than twenty years old. It will be interesting to learn the present-day survey participants' feelings about male-female relationships.

Although there hasn't been much research conducted on cross-gender friendships, what we do have would intimate that men find it more difficult to have cross-gender friendships than women. In 2012, William Bradley, a professor who taught a human sexuality course at Columbia College, commented on the Wisconsin study. He stated that, "Reproduction and sexual attraction are built into male genes and their egos. I think men are always looking for sexual liaisons. Men are predatory. Men are pigs. I mean that in a gentle way." Is Mr. Bradley on to something, or is he just a traitor to his gender? If Bradley really knows what he's talking about, then the question of a man being just friends with a woman instead becomes for the man a question of, "Why can't we be more than friends?"

Many times, a writer has to sift through a voluminous amount of material when searching for quantifiable information on a topic. However, the opposite was true when I searched for data on cross-gender friendships. My searches kept identifying fictional cross-gender friendships in movies and books but came up with a dearth of real-life examples. There are never-ending accounts of same-gender friendships, but I could use the fingers on my hand to keep track of the number of cross-gender friendships. It's sometimes said that what's left unspoken carries as much weight as what is spoken. In this case, it would seem that the paucity of narratives recounting examples of cross-gender friendships demonstrate the inherent difficulties of these relationships.

While doing my research, I suddenly realized that the answers to "How important is a woman's looks in your attraction to her?" should be mulled to correctly understand our men's responses to our question of "Do you think that a man can be 'just' friends with a woman?" Both men and women in our survey ranked a woman's good looks highly in a man's attraction to her. Does this mean that some of our men who said that yes, they could be just friends with a woman would change their answer if the question was worded, "Do you think that a man can be 'just' friends with a SEXY, BEAUTIFUL woman?" Hopefully, their answers won't change, but I tend to be a little cynical about some aspects of sexual attraction. Meanwhile, here are the men's responses to the question, "Can you be 'just' friends with a woman?"

MEN'S RESPONSES

JUST FRIENDS?	PERCENTAGE
Yes	70
No	14
It Depends	13
I don't know	3

Some of the male respondent's comments below indicate a hesitancy to establish cross-sex friendships because it might cause an issue with their romantic partner. Other comments note a woman's appearance as a determining factor in a friendship with a man.

- "Wife gets jealous."
- "Yes, but it's tough unless you find them completely unattractive, or they have some other major flaw."
- "I can't. I don't want no fake indiscretions being placed on my character. I sadly have very little trust of most women today."
- "Yes, can change though. Depends on circumstances, can evolve into more by one or both parties."
- "Yes, just someone to talk to."
- "If she is ugly."
- "Isn't that what women really want, just to be friends? I would still be friends with her even if I wanted more. How else can I spend time with her."
- "Yes, just like anyone. Although I will at some point imagine sex with a woman who is a friend, but that doesn't mean it must be acted on or given more than a cursory consideration."

Some of the men's comments indicate the possibility that simmering sexual desires hide beneath the surface of their platonic friendships with women. Do you think that our female survey respondents have correctly guessed whether the male respondents could be just friends with a woman?

WOMEN'S RESPONSES

JUST FRIENDS?	PERCENTAGE
Yes	63
No	24
It Depends	10
I don't know	3

Our female respondents' answers were pretty close to our male's answers. It seems that much of the wantonness between men and women that marked the days of Sodom and Gomorrah is truly a thing of the past. However, some of the female respondents' comments below are a little disconcerting.

- "Not at all, they all think with the wrong head."
- "No, because women get easily and quickly attached."
- "Yes, otherwise everyone would be sleeping with everyone all the time."
- "No, men are whores."
- "Yes, some men can be decent human beings, but it's rare."
- "Sometimes this can be a dangerous dance at times, though."
- "Yes, not all people are sexy."
- "No, all my male friends say they have an intention."
- "I think that men and women can be friends, especially if the man is gay. Gay men are the best friends a girl can have."
- "Yes, if they are homosexual."
- "A good man can."
- "Yes, but they secretly want more."
- "Yes, smart men can be."

Our female respondents' answers can be best summarized by saying that women believe that a man can be friends with a woman if the man is good, smart, homosexual and, oh yes, the woman can't be sexy. On the other hand, our survey has established that men can, in the right circumstances, keep their sexual fantasies in check long enough to be friends with a woman. We can breathe a sigh of relief over the possibility that men and women can be platonic friends.

Our next question will tell us whether men are comfortable being treated by female medical practitioners, or whether we should worry about them ripping the doctor's clothes off during an examination?

CHAPTER 10

ARE YOU NUTS: A FEMALE DOCTOR?

I'd like you to ask yourself the following questions: Do you think that female or male doctors spend more time listening to their patients? Are patient mortality rates in emergency rooms dependent on the gender of the physician? Does the gender of the physician have any bearing on the outcome of a patient's treatment? Are shared experiences important in psychotherapy? And finally, does a therapist's gender influence issues of transference and avoidance during psychotherapy? I'm going to give you some time to ponder the answers to these questions while we move on to see what Jim, Buddy, and Noah have to say about being treated by a female doctor, psychiatrist, or psychologist.

Jim believes in using specialists. He knows the extra effort that it takes to become an expert in your field. To attain an executive level in his job, he has had to be tested and licensed to prove his financial expertise. He would never think of asking an electrician to install new plumbing pipes in his home, so he can't understand why he wouldn't expect to be medically treated by the top specialists in their field. He has an internist, cardiologist, urologist, and dermatologist. He's always maintained that the gender of his doctors was not an issue for him. However, with the exception of physicians specializing in pediatrics, obstetrics, gynecology, and adolescent psychiatry, the medical specialty field is dominated by men.

Jim explains to Buddy and Noah. "If I'm going to have a triple bypass operation, I want the most experienced doctor to operate on me. It only makes sense that the most experienced doctor is the best, and many times that doctor who's been around the block more than a few times is a man. I don't think that this is gender bias. My thinking is based on the same reasoning when I choose my internist. Most people don't stop to think about the importance of this primary care physician. If this doctor misses something when I come in for an evaluation, it could mean the difference between life and death. Although I've read that women now make up more than 51 percent of students at US medical schools, according to a 2019 study in the *Journal of the American Medical Association,* the consensus among doctors is that women should confine themselves to practicing family medicine. Family medicine focuses on the social unit of the family while internal medicine treats adults and must include significant experience in each of its subspecialties. I'm not being prejudiced against women if even doctors themselves think that women should modify their leadership aspirations. Sure, I'd have a female doctor treat me if my problem was something simple like a sore throat. As far as my mental health, I don't think that a woman can possibly understand a man's viewpoint on certain things. I need to have a feeling of alliance with a therapist. It's important that I know that the therapist has possibly shared what I'm experiencing. I don't believe that it's possible for a woman therapist to have this alliance."

Buddy grins as he starts to speak. "I'm fascinated by what Jim just said because my friend basically slammed the women in his life by classifying female doctors to a secondary status to male doctors. A while back, I remember Jim saying that his daughter wanted to become a scientist. Does the limitations that he outlined for female doctors also apply to his daughter's role as a scientist? Will she have to constrain her discoveries to simple matters? At least I'm consistent when I give my thoughts about women. I know that some people might think that I'm rough around the edges, but I don't dance around the issues. My problem with women doctors isn't that I doubt their abilities. I think when hormones were given out that I was rewarded with an extra dose of testosterone. Although some men might have the reverse issue, I've had many situations in which I'll suddenly have a spontaneous erection. Although, I'd like to think it's because I'm such a manly man, I've read some stuff about this and apparently it happens to many men. Regardless, even though I have relatively few inhibitions, some men might be embarrassed by what might be construed as their body's manifestation of lustful thoughts. While you two might think that I'd get a kick out of something like this happening, I don't fool around when I'm in a doctor's office, and we're talking about my health."

Buddy continues. "Something else that ticks me off is how some female doctors will bring a chaperone into the examining room with them. It's like they think that I'm going to suddenly grope them or something. The whole scenario seems unnatural to me. Men should be treated by men and women by women, and that goes for therapy too. I don't want to have to watch my words for vulgarity or try to express myself in a gentlemanly way because I'm confiding in a woman therapist. How am I supposed to feel comfortable revealing some of my more prurient thoughts about things that most women don't understand?"

Noah isn't surprised by Jim's or Buddy's feelings about female doctors. However, their comments make him feel a bit superior. He likes to think that his education has made him more gentle and sophisticated. And when it comes to female physicians and therapists, he knows they have superior patient-centered skills. He realizes that he might be guilty of stereotyping women by generalizing their attributes, but generally speaking he thinks that nurturing and compassion are more pronounced in women. He tells his friends, "These traits are considered so important that I know of several medical schools that are teaching communication skills to male physicians. I'm a pretty modest guy, and I don't like to expose my body needlessly. However, if I have a choice between a female doctor who pays careful attention to what I tell her and a male doctor who keeps looking at his watch, I'll pick the female doctor. I think it would be crazy to be embarrassed by conversations with a therapist. Unless I was a sadistic serial killer, there is nothing that I could confess to a therapist that he or she hasn't heard before. Actually, maybe my therapist has treated a serial killer, but that doesn't affect me one way or the other. I'll check the credentials of my doctors, but I otherwise trust their knowledge as professionals regardless of their gender."

Our three men have very definitive thoughts on whether they would be comfortable being treated by a female medical or mental health physician. Buddy's inability to cast aside his sexual urges when treated by a female doctor points out an inability to distinguish the difference between a female professional and a female as a love interest. Perhaps the biblical warning to male doctors that it's wrong for men to see and touch private parts of any sexually mature woman who is not his wife is based on a similar belief. According to both Buddy and the Bible, men apparently can't control their lustfulness when either they or a woman is unclothed.

Throughout history, there are many reasons used to discriminate against women in the medical profession, and to explain why men aren't comfortable with female doctors. But before we look at some of these reasons, I want to share with you some research data that provides objective answers to the questions I asked you to think about in the first paragraph of this chapter.

There are many subjective reasons that influence a person's choice of a physician, although we'd probably all agree that the avoidance of death or spending your days in a mental institution should be at the top of your list. There's a general consensus that you'll have a better chance of being diagnosed correctly if you have a woman primary care physician, as studies indicate that woman doctors listen more than their male counterparts. The *New York Times* cited Dr. Don Barr, a professor at Stanford Medical School, who stated that female primary care doctors waited an average of three minutes before interrupting a patient, while male doctors averaged forty-seven seconds. This may seem inconsequential unless the doctor misses a life-changing symptom that the patient is disclosing. It's sort of like shooting at a target blindfolded.

In 2016, a Harvard study of one-and-a-half million hospitalized Medicare patients showed that these patients were less likely to die if their doctor was a woman. A 2018 study of more than 580,000 heart patients admitted to emergency rooms in Florida supports the results of the Harvard study. The 2018 study showed that mortality rates were lower if the attending physician was female. Based on these two studies, it seems like a no-brainer for a patient to choose a woman physician if given a choice between a male and a female physician. However, in past decades there were very few female physicians. Women who wanted to enter the medical field became nurses.

Now, as of 2021, 50.6 percent of primary care physicians in the United States are women. Since they have entered the medical field after many of their male counterparts, their medical knowledge considers the latest findings and processes. Studies also indicate that female doctors follow the latest clinical guidelines and evidence-based practice. They are known to order more tests to provide better preventive services, and they often offer psychosocial counseling. These practices can only enhance the chances of recovery for a patient.

When considering the choice of whether to use a female medical practitioner, many men might ask themselves, "How can a woman possibly understand my insecurities about not being able to get an erection?" Men are not alone in this concern over the lack of shared experiences in their medical treatment by doctors of the opposite gender. Women also bemoan the thought that a male doctor will attribute their complaints to female idiosyncrasies that the physician attributes to out-of-control hormones, stress, or a vivid imagination.

Gender bias is prevalent among both men and women. Apprehension about being treated by medical professionals of the opposite gender can be overcome by considering the doctor-patient interaction an opportunity to get the perspective of the opposite gender. Understanding this perspective will hopefully result in more comfort and trust by both male and female patients. On the other hand, because masculinity often equates with strength and emotional restraint, men might feel a sense of shame to open up about their perceived weaknesses to a woman.

As we've noted there are numerous reasons why a physician's gender may be a consideration in the treatment of physical ailments, but is gender important in the treatment of mental conditions? Most of us are familiar with the concept of transference in which a patient transfers feelings such as anger or love to the therapist. Obviously, if a man has been tremendously hurt by a woman, it's possible that he might transfer his hatred toward women to a female therapist. Men and women dealing with sexual abuse also might find it uncomfortable to open up about certain sensitive issues with a therapist of the opposite gender. In time, a good therapist should be able to use the patient's transference and avoidance as tools to address the serious problems affecting the patient.

As we continue our search to discover if men are comfortable being treated by female physicians and therapists, I'd like to remind you to keep in mind your personal thoughts on this subject as we probe the past.

YESTERDAY

There are virtually no narratives referencing women doctors during biblical times. However, according to the Hebrew and Jewish studies scholar Azila Reisenberg there are several hieroglyphs in the Bible that provide visual evidence of the existence of midwives. For example, in Exodus 1:4, a woman is depicted sitting over two stones to deliver a baby. The stones are positioned high enough off the floor for a midwife to be able to reach under the woman and catch the baby. Since women's principal role in society was to be fruitful and multiply, the midwife held an important position.

One of the first documented narratives proving the existence of women physicians is described in the story of Merit-Ptah who lived in

Egypt in 2700 BC. Merit-Ptah was the first female physician known by name and was the royal court's chief physician. It can be assumed that in this important role, her duties involved treating men as well as women. For her to attain such a lofty position, men must have felt comfortable being treated by her.

There is, however, some controversy about the validity of the story of Merit-Ptah because there is evidence that she might actually be a fictional character. The tomb of Akhethetep, a high dignitary during ancient Egyptian times, notes that the story of Merit-Ptah is actually his mother's story. Her name was Peseshet. On Akhethetep's tomb he identifies his mother as the overseer of physicians. The importance of this narrative, regardless of whether Merit-Ptah or Peseshet was the first female physician, is that there is proof that female doctors not only existed in Ancient Egypt and were also lauded.

In addition to these indications that men accepted female doctors in Ancient Egypt, there are many pictures on tombs depicting them performing surgery. However, it wasn't until 1832 that women began studying medicine at the Egyptian Royal Medical School. Unfortunately, such an enlightened attitude toward female doctors didn't exist everywhere in ancient times. During the fifteenth century BC, the Hittites in Turkey believed that diseases were created by evil spirits, and female healers excised them with magic rituals. It also was believed that a woman's chastity was impaired if she practiced hands-on medicine. It would probably be a good guess that if it was a matter of life or death, that men would have eagerly swallowed the herbs and potions that these women provided and cast aside their feelings of discomfort about their healer being a woman.

In fourth century BC Athens, the midwife Agnodice made quite a name for herself as a talented healer. The only problem with her practicing her skills was that it was illegal in Athens for a woman to practice medicine. Nonetheless, Agnodice was so dedicated to her craft that she disguised herself as a man. However, the one source (Hyginus) for our story of Agnodice does not make it clear whether she treated men as well as women. Therefore, we can't say with certainty whether men would have welcomed her treatment if they knew that she was a woman.

During this time in Greece, many women were dying because they were too embarrassed to be treated by a man. Agnodice wanted to help women, so she revealed to them that she was not actually a man. She became very popular with her patients, but regrettably the male doctors were jealous of her success. The men still believed that Agnodice was a man, so they turned her into the authorities for seducing women. She went to trial, where she disclosed it to the court where her true gender was revealed. Her women patients protested in support of Agnodice, and because of her, the law against women practicing medicine in Athens was repealed.

―

THE ANCIENT ROMANS were even less progressive than the Greeks in their view of women practicing medicine. They stated their belief that women were not suited to be physicians because their physiology made them irrational. They didn't recognize the dichotomy between their rejection of female doctors with their worship of numerous goddesses of healing. Their comfort with female healers apparently only applied to female healing deities.

Regardless of the general view of men during ancient Roman times, there were still a few powerful men during that time who believed in equality between the sexes. In 530 AD, Emperor Justinian passed a law establishing that men and women doctors should be equal in all ways. The ladies must have loved Justinian.

There were no medical schools until the ninth century, when the *Schola Medica Salernitana* at Salerno, Italy opened. Up until then, much of what a person learned about medicine was through apprenticeships. Because most men didn't think that it was suitable for women to become doctors, it was very difficult for women to convince men to be their mentors. However, many women, such as the renowned gynecologist Trota and the surgeon and eye specialist Costanza Caalenda, attended the Salerno medical school. There was even a classification of healers known as the *Mulieres Salernitanae*. They were women who used empirical methods to diagnose illnesses and then submitted their remedies to the school's doctors for implementation. From this example, it appears that in ninth century Italy, men acknowledged women's medical wisdom.

By the thirteenth century, the influence of the Salerno medical school had diminished, and it was declared that a degree from the University of Paris was considered the only valid medical education in Europe. However, women doctors continued to learn most of their skills informally from a family member. So, it's understandable that men, and probably some

women too, didn't feel comfortable being treated by a self-educated woman. Before too long, women practicing medicine were being fined or imprisoned for treating patients without a university degree. In 1325, the outrage even reached the Vatican. Pope John XXII forbid the practice of medicine by women without formal medical training. He warned that these women were doing the work of the devil by practicing witchcraft. However, now that you think about it, women also should have felt uncomfortable when they put their lives in the hands of female physicians who, for the most part, lacked the training given to their male counterparts.

—

SURPRISINGLY, EVEN THOUGH for many eras there was resistance to the idea of women formally practicing medicine, twenty-four surgeries were performed by women surgeons in Naples, Italy between 1273 and 1410. There is no information on whether the outcomes of those surgeries were successful. We do know that women were sometimes accepted as scholars in the field of medicine. For instance, in the twelfth century, there were women like Hildegard of Bingen who wrote medical textbooks about numerous diseases, and these textbooks were used by male physicians in their practices.

The Renaissance was known as a period of rebirth. Unfortunately, however, for women physicians, it was the end of their shaky acceptance into the world of medicine. The general consensus among men was that women were spiritually and mentally inferior. They believed that physiologically a woman's body was a poor imitation of a male body because the uterus was simply an inverted version of the male penis. Therefore, men saw females as a second-rate version of a male doctor. Just as in the fourteenth century, women who practiced medicine were again accused of being witches and often were executed. By the end of the sixteenth century, even obstetrical care was delegated to male physicians only, and remained so until the twentieth century.

THERE WERE RARE instances in the seventeenth century of women attaining prominence in the medical field. In Switzerland, midwife Marie Colinet of Bern was taught surgery by her surgeon husband. She made a name for herself as a surgeon when, in addition to performing obstetrical operations and cesarean sections, she wired together the ribs of an injured man. Kupeli Saliha Hatun of Turkey performed hernia surgery on both men and women. It's also interesting to note that although women were generally prohibited from becoming physicians during the Renaissance, they were responsible for identifying and processing medicinal herbs and creating various remedies. Many of these women were nuns living in Italy, including Orsola Fontebuoni who worked in her convent pharmacy and could claim the members of the Medici court among her patrons. It's strange that men had no qualms about swallowing the medicines created by women, yet they didn't think that they should be physicians.

WHEN AMERICA DECLARED its independence from England it prided itself on being a more enlightened country than its parent. However, in its early years, the American colonies lagged behind Europe in the establishment of medical schools. It wasn't until 1765 that the University of Pennsylvania's medical school was founded. If you haven't already guessed, women were prohibited from attending this medical school.

It would be eighty-two years after that founding before a woman was permitted to attend an American medical school. In 1847 Elizabeth Blackwell became the first. She had initially been rejected by all the schools to which she applied until she was accepted at Geneva Medical School in New York. However, the male sentiment against training women physicians was still so widespread at Geneva that the admissions department flippantly decided to let the male students vote on whether Blackwell should be accepted. They were confident that the men would never vote to admit her. However, as a practical joke, the men decided to vote for her admittance. In 1857, she founded the New York Infirmary for Women and Children. In 1867, ten years after the infirmary opened, a medical college for women was added. Training and experience would now be available for women hoping to become physicians. I bet that her male peers at Geneva Medical School were choking with resentment over her perseverance.

Woman continued to slowly make their way in medicine. In 1862, Ann Preston founded the Woman's Medical College in Pennsylvania and became the first woman to become dean of a medical school. She encountered tremendous resistance from other male medical professionals, and the Philadelphia County Medical Society went so far as to formally object to the practice of medicine by women. Things only got worse when Preston took a group of about thirty of her female medical students to attend a general clinic at the Pennsylvania

Hospital. Preston noted that upon leaving the hospital, "We were actually stoned by those so-called gentleman" (Alsop pp.54-55).

This male reaction to the idea of female doctors wasn't that unusual. A few years earlier, in 1847, Harriot K. Hunt was the first woman to apply to Harvard Medical School and was denied a seat when the all-male class threatened to leave if women or Blacks were admitted. There was even an article criticizing Hunt published in the *New York Times* in 1858. It stated that her desire to practice medicine was because she was "one of the dozen women in the United States who pine because nature did not make them men." Obviously, many men in the nineteenth century not only felt uncomfortable with female doctors, but they also thought that they were an aberration of nature.

Ann Preston and Elizabeth Blackwell weren't the only women to experience the wrath of men when they tried to enter the medical world in the mid-1800s. Sophia Jex Blake began studying medicine at the University of Edinburgh. She and six other women, who became known as the Edinburg 7, encountered violence when they arrived at the school to take an anatomy exam. They were met by a mob of more than two hundred men who shouted insults and threw mud and rubbish at them. The women continued attending classes until members of the medical faculty appealed to the courts to address what they thought was an outrageous situation. Unbelievably, in 1873, the courts ruled that the women shouldn't have been allowed to take the course and that any degrees that were granted to them could be withdrawn. Women were prohibited from graduating. Blake was finally awarded an MD degree at the University of Berne and later founded the Edinburg School of Medicine for Women, and she helped establish the London School of Medicine for Women. Blake refused to give up her goals. On the other hand, one has to be a bit perplexed by her comment about the need for women doctors. In a medical pamphlet she wrote that "Women are not properly attended in their confinement because the idea of employing a man was so extremely repugnant to them." Her words signified that men of her generation weren't the only ones who were uneasy about being treated by doctors of the opposite gender.

To best sum up the general attitude of men toward women physicians in the nineteenth century, consider the words of Edward H. Clarke, a professor of medicine at Harvard. He wrote in 1875 in his book *Sex In Education*, "When women become educated, it negatively affects their health leaving them with puny bodies, weak digestion, and constipated bowels." All signs point to the conclusion that men were uncomfortable being patients of women physicians during that time.

If you wanted a woman therapist in the nineteenth century, you had to wait until 1894 to find one. Margaret Washburn was the first woman to get her PhD in psychology in 1894. This was a great achievement for a woman of her generation. Even though female therapists were being recognized for their skills, not everyone was on board with granting these accolades. An example of this was Mary Whiton Calkins. She was refused a doctorate degree by Harvard and yet went on to become the first woman president of the Psychological Association in 1905.

TODAY

You'd be wrong if you thought that in the twentieth century, the male mindset changed toward women physicians. In 1905, Dr. F.W. Van Dyke, the president of the Oregon State Medical Society, stated, "Hard study killed sexual desire in women, took away their beauty, brought on hysteria, neurasthenia, dyspepsia, astigmatism, and dysmenorrhea. Educated women could not bear children with ease because study arrested the development of the pelvis" (Bullough and Voght, pp.74-75). A woman would think twice before working herself to death if she believed Dr. Van Dyke's admonishments that her hard study would result in her suffering from ailments ranging from indigestion to imperfections in the curvature of her eyes. Despite these misplaced cautions, women proved to be irrepressible in their professional aspirations and refused to have their dreams thwarted.

During World War I, there was a great need for doctors. However, even though women physicians were commissioned by the military, they were treated much differently than their male counterparts. The contracts that women signed to practice medicine in the military didn't include military status or benefits. Nonetheless, there were many female doctors who offered their medical services to the US military but were rejected because of their gender. France, however, was eager to get help from them. The National American Women Suffrage Association joined forces with four of these female doctors to form an all-women's medical team to staff hospitals in France. Hardly any information exists about this team other than to say that they were welcomed with open arms in France.

This distinction between female and male physicians was also noticeable in the paucity of women in medical leadership positions. In the 1970s, women were restricted to practicing primary care based on the assumption that women didn't do well in technically oriented surgical fields. Even today, this false assumption continues to affect women physicians as evidenced in a 2017 report by the Association of Medical Colleges that states that women make up only a quarter of ten surgical specialties (aamc.org).

It wasn't until the late twentieth century that women attained any status in the medical field. In 1988 Gertrude Belle Elion received the Nobel Prize for creating drugs to treat kidney transplant rejection, leukemia, herpes, and AIDS. Although she was a biochemist and not a physician, her work saved many lives. It's probably okay to surmise that men would feel comfortable taking these lifesaving drugs even if they knew they were created by a woman.

Perhaps the most prestigious example of a woman's success in the medical field is demonstrated in the life of Antonia Novello. In 1990, Novello was appointed US surgeon general by George H.W. Bush, a groundbreaking precedent. She was the first woman and Latino to serve in this medical leadership position, and without male resistance.

Women physicians in modern times have broken through most of the barriers, gaining widespread acceptance and admiration for their growing list of accomplishments.

Dr. Virginia Apgar is credited with inventing a process called the Apgar score that reduced infant mortality. Most men probably wouldn't hesitate to have their male son treated by Dr. Apgar. Dr. Maria Siemionow was the transplant surgeon who led the team at the Cleveland Clinic in 2008 that performed a near-total face transplant. Although many men might not be aware of her contribution unless they had cataract surgery, Dr. Patricia Era Bath was awarded a patent for the development of the laserphaco probe, a medical device that helps restore sight to people who are almost blind. As we can see, women are no longer confined to practicing pediatrics, obstetrics, and gynecology.

It's clear and undeniable that women have made great strides in equalizing the medical playing field with men. As noted, they now comprise more than half of the students in degree-granting medical schools. Women have even become the dominant gender in the field of mental health. In centuries past, it was believed that the cause of mental illness was that someone was cursed, possessed, or suffering from hysteria, and sadly, no therapists were being trained to address these issues. The common cure consisted of purging, bloodletting, exorcisms, and isolation. The first mental hospital in the United States wasn't established until 1752. The fitting nickname for these hospitals was *snake pits*, indicative of the horrendous conditions existing in these mental health facilities at the time. A patient's priority wasn't the gender of his therapist, it was getting out of the hospital alive.

Female mental health physicians were almost nonexistent at the time. Any mental health treatments performed by women were intertwined with religious and spiritual practices. Mystics such as Margery Kempe wrote about her struggle with mental challenges in *The Book of Margery Kempe*. Some female physicians attempted to take a holistic approach in the treatment of their female patients by addressing any mental issues, but these physicians confined much of their practice to women.

There hardly is anyone who doesn't recognize the name Sigmund Freud or hasn't heard of Freud's theory of penis envy. However, there are probably very few people who have heard of psychiatrist Karen Horney, who is credited with founding feminist psychology. She challenged Freud about his theories on the inherent psychological differences between men and women and coined the term *womb envy* to express the reason behind some of the issues in male-female relationships. If Freud and Horney are to be believed, the oppositional nature of these two theories could contribute to a man's or woman's hesitancy to undergo treatment with a therapist of the opposite gender. Perhaps the gender of a therapist wouldn't matter if the issue was a universal concern to both men and women.

The book, *On Death and Dying* by Dr. Elizabeth Kubler Ross, outlined the five stages of grief. It's difficult to imagine any man being uncomfortable accepting treatment by Dr. Ross if his mental health issues revolved around death and dying. The universality of this subject negates most gender influences.

The American Psychological Association conducted a report in 2017 that showed that 75 percent of psychology graduate students are female. This means that whether he likes it or not, in the present day a man probably doesn't have much choice in choosing the gender of his mental health therapist.

Understandably, if most psychology graduate students are female, it's not surprising that women comprise 70 percent of therapy professions for which the average salary is $74,987. This relatively low salary for a top-tier professional is often cited as a reason why men shy away from this field. It's surprising that women aren't also concerned about the salary since there are an increasing number of single moms responsible for supporting a family. Regardless of the reason for the dearth of male therapists, this scarcity results in men often finding themselves in treatment with a woman therapist. However, the good news is that research shows that today's men are agreeable to treatment by female therapists. Our friends Jim and Buddy are out of step. Now it's time to learn what our survey respondents have to say about a man's comfort in being treated by a woman physician or therapist.

MEN'S RESPONSES

COMFORTABLE WITH WOMAN PHYSICIANS	PERCENTAGE
Yes	84
No	11
I don't know	4
It Depends	1

The men's overwhelming consensus that they'd be comfortable being treated by a female physician or therapist is an encouraging sign, suggesting that they believe that women are as capable as men in the medical field. Here are some of their comments.

- "Yes, because they are very tender."
- "Yes, but not for genitourinary exams."
- "Yes, as long as they fix my problem."
- "I've had female doctors in the past and they were okay. But I'd rather see a male doctor if I need to talk about intimacy issues."
- "Yes, women are more empathetic and caring."
- "Yes, I don't mean to sound sexist, but I would rather have a woman examine my body than a dude. Same goes for my brain."

That last comment is a little ambiguous as it seems to infer a sexual association that might imply our respondent gets a little more than comfort in his treatment by a female doctor. Our female respondents seem to have a different take on a man's comfort in being treated by a female physician or therapist.

WOMEN'S RESPONSES

COMFORTABLE WITH WOMEN PHYSICIANS	PERCENTAGE
Yes	40
No	30
It depends	22
I don't know	8

Our female respondents' answers noticeably lack the enthusiasm reflected in our male respondents' declaration that they are comfortable when undergoing treatment with a female physician or therapist. Some of the women also are a little caustic in their comments as seen below.

- "No, they don't want a woman to see them in that vulnerable way."
- "No, because she'd make him feel inferior by having a woman give him advice."
- "Some would, some would think she's inferior, either to themselves or to an imaging male provider."
- "Yes, they would feel less vulnerable."
- "Yes, because he could check her out and screw her in his mind."
- "I think that some would feel intimidated by a woman in power."
- "No, he would be fearful of vulnerability and of a woman telling him what to do."
- "Yes, because men are arrogant pigs and being a doctor just means that women are serving them."
- "I suspect most would prefer a man. Women are often their problem, so why would woman solve their problems?"

At least our last respondent injected a bit of humor into her answer. Many of the women's comments reference a man's fear of appearing vulnerable and yet this wasn't reflected in the answers from the male respondents.

Our next question touches on a man's perception of a woman's primary role in society and whether that role is to raise the children and take care of the home.

CHAPTER 11

THE GREAT DEBATE:
BEYOND APRONS AND LULLABIES

A close female friend of mine has a very demanding job that would seemingly make her look forward to getting some relaxation on the weekends. However, she confided in me that she actually dreaded weekends because she would then have to face the endless duties that come with motherhood. Weekends also are when she catches up on household chores that she couldn't get to during the week. This friend is not a single mom. She has a successful husband who thinks that he is being progressive because he asks her from time to time if there's anything that he can do to *help* her. He believes that his offer of help is a magnanimous gesture as he obviously thinks that childcare and homemaking are a woman's duty. It never enters his mind that maybe he should be equally responsible for the care of his children and management of the family's home. After hearing some of Jim, Buddy, and Noah's opinions about women in earlier chapters, most of you can now probably surmise what their sentiments will be about a woman's responsibility for childcare and housework, although maybe one of them will surprise you.

When Jim was growing up, both his mother and sister could have served as a prototype of a dutiful wife and mother whose sole purpose centered on her family. Jim assumed that his wife also believed that this traditional role fulfilled her destiny, until the day that she told him that she was going to work outside the home. Therefore, Jim never gave a second thought to the possibility that the female executives working with him might also be mothers and wives, and that their second shift would just begin when they got home from work.

Before Jim married, he paid a cleaning woman to handle many household tasks. He expected her to make sure that he'd never open his refrigerator and see green mold on his food. Now that Jim was focusing on family and household responsibilities, he realized that he was a bit entitled and that for most of his life all of his needs were attended to. He told Buddy and Noah, "I can finally admit to myself that I was happy with my distorted illusion of a woman's role. Who wouldn't be happy with never having to scrub a toilet or change a dirty diaper? If I wanted to be totally forthright, I'd have to admit that if the women in my life were satisfied adopting my mom's and sister's roles, I wouldn't dissuade them. This probably means that I'm selfish. Although I would be proud if my wife and daughter attain their professional goals, I wouldn't want that to happen if it was at my expense."

Buddy turned to his two friends and said, "Jim just took the words out of my mouth. Hell, if a woman can become a big shot in the workplace, it wouldn't bother me at all as long as she didn't neglect her homemaking and childcare duties. As a matter of fact, I'd be glad if her bringing home the bread meant that I'd have less pressure to work hard at my job. Although some people might think I'm a bit of a slob, I don't like seeing roaches running all over my kitchen counters. Everybody knows that a kid needs somebody to take care of him or her during the first few years of their lives. If I ever marry, I'd be willing to support my wife and kids so she could do her childcaring and household duties. If she's not happy with what I can give her and wants to work to get more then she better be prepared to come home from work and also take care of the kids and home."

Noah and Jane both acknowledge that climbing the academic ladder is an important goal in both their lives. The focus on their careers has made them delay marriage until they've attained their career goals. They both exhibit a touch of OCD when it comes to their expectations for the condition of their home. Nothing less than pristine is acceptable to them. Unfortunately, neither Noah or Jane want to spare any of their time performing housework when they could use this time achieving their professional goals or enjoying their leisure time together. Noah explains to his friends that, "Jane and I are by no means wealthy, but we'd rather pay someone to clean our home than fight over who should do the chores. Although I have seniority over Jane with my professorial position at the university, I know how serious she is about her advancement. When we started dating, I never told her that she was more suited for housework than me because she was a woman, so why would I change my beliefs now that we live together. If you think about it, I'm probably more suited to do the manual labor required because I'm physically stronger than Jane."

NOAH ADDS, "IF we ever decide to marry and have a child, ideally one of us would want to stay at home during the child's early years. However, that doesn't necessarily mean that person would be Jane. Depending on our career trajectory at the time, I might be the one staying home for a while. After all, you need both a man and a woman to make a baby so why would I expect Jane to be the caretaker. If neither of us are available for childcare, there are many wonderful nannies we could pay to help us out."

Noah's feelings about a woman's role in childcare and household duties probably has a lot of the woman reading this vigorously clapping in appreciation. On the other hand, I was a little taken aback by Jim's admission, although it was his honesty that most amazed me. Many of us might share Jim's feelings about making himself a priority, but we're rarely as candid as he is in announcing his perspective on the subject. Frequently, women who have no desire to be homemakers or mothers believe that revealing this to others will make them appear unfeminine. Conversely, many women prefer to stay at home and raise their children but in today's *Lean In* environment, these women often keep their thoughts to themselves.

Our three men have given us their thoughts on this question so now it's time to again look at men's attitudes in the past and the present day to see if they think that it's primarily a woman's responsibility to raise children and take care of the home.

YESTERDAY

More than 90 percent of people named in the Hebrew Bible are men, so it's a little difficult to learn about the lives of women during biblical times. Passages such as Proverbs 31 suggest that a woman's work was truly never done. The words, "She selects wool and flax and works with eager hand and . . . She gets up while it is still night-she provides" definitely underscore a woman's responsibility in the home during biblical times. To make sure that we understand the managerial role of the man in the family, 1 Timothy 3-4 states that "An overseer must manage his own household well and keep his children under control, with complete dignity." The addition of the words *complete dignity* makes it clear that men's duties in biblical times couldn't be subservient to a woman's role. This meant that you'd find very few men sweeping the packed dirt floors of their homes.

The ancient Celtic culture during the Iron Age in Britain demonstrated a shift in a woman's responsibility for the home and children as clans took the place of nuclear families. Children were seldom raised by their own parents but were fostered by other members of the clan who were often male relatives. Women were considered equal to men and could own property, choose their own husbands, and even lead in war. Any man expressing the view that their future wife should stay home and raise the children would probably find himself single for a long time.

In ancient Greek times, the pendulum swung back to the biblical belief that women were solely responsible for raising children. In addition, they had the duties of weaving and sewing the family's clothes. Many of the more mundane, arduous tasks of housekeeping were delegated to the female slaves. If a woman was part of the lower classes, she had the same status as a slave and was expected to assume all of the laborious tasks delegated to the slave class.

The women of ancient Rome had the same responsibilities as the women of ancient Greece. There were some differences between the two civilizations such as the elimination of gendered spaces in the Roman home that were *de rigueur* in Greece. Roman women now had the whole run of the house. However, Roman men had the final say on the really important things in the family. The power of the father even extended to his right to order the death of an unwanted infant. When a child was born it was placed on the ground by the midwife. The father would then either accept it by picking it up or leave it outside to die of exposure. He could also decide who his children would marry or whether they would be sold into slavery. If we consider that responsibility means having legal and moral accountability for something or someone, then we'd have to say that in ancient Rome, fathers had the ultimate responsibility for their children.

The Romans created the position of male nutritor, a male nurse who was either a freeman or slave and who would accompany a child into public spaces that prohibited entry to lower-class women. Wealthy families also had full-time nurses who raised the children along with mothers. Apparently, Romans were proponents of shared childcaring duties, as long as the sharing wasn't done with the fathers.

In early centuries, Japan was a matriarchal society in which women were encouraged to act as rulers. By the late sixth century, these powers declined as Buddhism declared that women were evil. The Edo period in Japan further eroded women's status in society and stated that women ruled in the house while men ruled everywhere else. This might not sound like such a bad deal unless you consider the extent of a man's power in Japan during the seventeenth and eighteenth centuries. Men could kill their wives for being lazy or disobedient. I bet those Japanese housewives really hustled to satisfy their husbands. A woman's power in her home was limited to what food to cook and how to care for her child. Legally, they had no rights. The Japanese saying, *Danshi-Chubo-Ni-Hairazu* meant that men should be ashamed to be found in the kitchen, which seems to sum up the attitude of Japanese men.

—

DURING MEDIEVAL TIMES in Europe, the Middle East, China, East Asia, and Africa, fathers participated in childrearing. However, this was managerial rather than hands-on care. The father would hire wet nurses and decide when the child should be weaned. Fathers were responsible for their son's education once they reached the age of seven. The aristocracy sent their sons to another noble house to be trained for knighthood. Those fathers with less means apprenticed their sons with another father, while peasant fathers educated their children themselves in their own homes. During this period, women were relieved of their childcare duties. Did the men think women were too incompetent to properly raise their children, or were they just progressive enough to share the work?

The Victorian era in Europe declared the perfect woman as the "angel of the household." Not all women were happy with this designation. Virginia Wolfe captured the attitude of many women during this time period in her words, "Killing the angel of the house was part of the occupation of a woman writer." It was easy to see why many women agreed with Wolf, considering that this angel probably was encouraged to have at least six children as well as cook and clean. Wealthier women had domestics whom she supervised, but even then, she was to limit her social activities to fifteen-to-twenty-minute visits. Poorer women could choose between becoming a nanny, factory worker, domestic or prostitute. However, this didn't excuse her from taking care of her own living quarters and children. Of course, regardless of her position in society, a woman had to remain pure because she was an *angel*. It took a war to change this idealized male version of the perfect woman.

TODAY

By 1914 the angel of the household was working in factories and nursing injured soldiers back to health. World War I had dramatically changed the lifestyle of both men and women. The Industrial Revolution shifted the places people lived from rural to city life, and women were now exposed to many things that they had been sheltered from in the past. The concept of the domestic angel had been based on a devotion to God. Many women became atheists to escape that ideology. Women now had options.

In the early part of the twentieth century, the working class didn't have white collar jobs. Instead, they brought piecework into their homes. There was about a 20 percent growth in the women's workforce between 1890 and 1940. However, women were still expected to be caretakers for the home, and children and fierce resistance was met with any mention of birth control. In the mid-twentieth century American fathers started to participate in childcare, mostly to be a pal to one's child or to help their wives. Men played with their children. Women worked for them.

In the post-World War II period, society promoted the idea that women found complete fulfillment in the domestic sphere. In 1963, Feminist Betty Friedan published her book, *The Feminine Mystique*, which was the name that she gave for the erroneous societal assumption that a woman's self-actualization and contentment came from taking care of the home and family. Her book refuted this fallacy, and it was a rallying cry for women to admit that they wanted more than this. Friedan argued in her book that women deserved to attain personal achievements.

There were many books written empowering woman during Friedan's time. However, some of these books promoted philosophies that demeaned instead of acknowledged women's abilities. Books such as *Fascinating Womanhood* by Helen Andelin, and *The Total Woman* by Marabel Morgan reinforced the traditional gender roles of female submissiveness and domesticity.

The introduction of what was called "scientific motherhood" didn't do much to alleviate a women's responsibility for childcare and housework. Instead, experts like Dr. Spock disempowered mothers. His advice declared that women were vessels who carried children, but a mother didn't always know best. In addition to having full responsibility for their children and homes, women now had to adhere to rigid guidelines. Spock's book *Baby and Child Care* became the Bible for all new mothers and shamed women who ignored its dictates. It was clear that not only was it a woman's responsibility to care for her children, but it had better be done according to Spock's directives.

THERE ARE STILL many books telling women how to care for their home and children. However, many women in the 1960s, '70s and '80s turned away from the June Cleaver perfect mom/housekeeper model. Instead, women showed appreciation for the sentiments expressed in the feminist call to Bury Mother's Day that was captured in a poster that appeared in Cleveland on Mother's Day in 1969. The Women's International Conspiracy from Hell (WITCH) was responsible for its message that said, "We want wages for every dirty toilet, every painful childbirth, every indecent assault, every cup of coffee, and every smile. And if we don't get what we want, then we will simply refuse to work any longer." The result? "Now you will rot in your own garbage." The message ends with "We want it in cash, retroactive and immediately. And we want all of it." This probably sounds pretty funny now that we're in modern times, and household and childcare responsibilities no longer rest solely on a woman's shoulders. But have things actually changed that much?

Picture this scenario. It's a tense moment in the negotiations between two national corporations regarding the terms of a pending acquisition. Suddenly, a ringtone from the lead attorney's cell phone interrupts the discussion. Thinking that it's an emergency, the attorney, who happens to be a woman, answers the call. It's her daughter who excitedly tells her, "Mom, I knew that you'd want to know that I just got an *A* in English." Mortified that someone overheard this exchange, the attorney quickly ends the call. This woman has succeeded in her profession, but her role as a mother is something that constantly intrudes into her professional life. It's possible, but unlikely, that this young girl would call her father at work with this news. Unless this woman has a full-time housekeeper, she probably starts her second work shift the minute that she opens the door to her home. Is this what it means to have it all?

Although things have evened out a bit in the household/childcare responsibilities between men and women, research indicates that women still have not gotten total relief from these duties. A Gallup poll in January of 2020 indicates that women still handle 51 percent of the main tasks in the home and do 50 percent of childcare. Although this sounds like a pretty even split of responsibilities, according to data from the Organization for Economic Cooperation and Development, women in the US spend about four hours a day on unpaid work, compared to about 2.5 hours for men. That's a big difference. This data also fails to indicate whether the men have taken substantial responsibility for child and home care because they truly believe it's part of their role in society, or that they resentfully perform these duties to maintain peace in the home.

Nonetheless, there is a light in the horizon that shines on some men who, regardless of this data, proudly stand up and declare that they are equally responsible for their family's care. The nonprofit organization National at Home Dad Network was founded in 2006. Its mission is to provide advocacy, community, education, and support for families where the fathers are primary caregivers for their children. It's the only nonprofit exclusively for stay at-home dads and has become so successful that they hold packed yearly conventions named HomeDad.com. We need to applaud them for their slogan, *Dad's Don't Babysit (It's Called Parenting)*. Now all we need is for someone to form an organization called Dads Who Mop and Vacuum, and most women in the world would be happy.

AT THIS POINT, we can't ignore the reality that there's a long way to go to balance the scale of men and women's responsibilities for childcare and housework. A 2018 study by Cerrato and Cifre states that men engage in over 50 percent more leisure time than women and that only 9 percent of men assume responsibility for meal prep, 10 percent for laundry, and 5 percent for cleaning. Regarding childcare, 9 percent take time off from work for a sick child, 9 percent to help with homework and 3 percent to organize their child's activities. These numbers confirm that as of 2018 women are primarily responsible for childcare and housework and suggest that men gladfully accept that premise. Let's see if our survey respondents agree.

The male respondents overwhelmingly rejected the data of the aforementioned research conducted by Cerrato and Cifre. Hopefully, since the statistics below are the results of an anonymous survey, we can trust the veracity of our male respondents. Either their answers are a sign that men are acknowledging the equal status of women and men as caregivers and homemakers, or our survey men are saying what they think women want to hear. Here are their answers to the question, Do you think that it's primarily a women's responsibility to raise children and/or take care of the home?

MEN'S RESPONSES

WOMAN RESPONSIBLE CHILDCARE/HOUSEKEEPING	PERCENTAGE
Yes	22
No	60
It Depends	12
I don't know	6

Most of the male respondents seem to have given a lot of thought to this question of parental responsibility for childcare and housekeeping, regardless of whether they believe that it's the sole responsibility of the female parent. The first comment might irritate some of our readers, but we can probably all agree that our male respondent carefully considered his answer. His response is quite lengthy, but I've included the entire comment as it represents the opinions of many of the men who answered yes to our question.

- "Yes, speaking biologically, historically, culturally, and innate to virtually all higher-level animals, the female takes care of the young. To assume a male should assume equal responsibility is both counter-productive and incredibly naive. A father cannot produce sustenance for the child, and he lacks the maternal instinct a female has for her children. This can be very easily seen across the animal kingdom, yet for some reason, modern media and current social mores imply it should not continue the way it has existed since the beginning of time."
- "No. A home is made of a family and every member of that family should contribute to the success of the household. If one person doesn't, the whole thing collapses."
- "Yes, children seem to need their mothers more than their fathers based on the nurturing involved."

- "No to both, but in my relationship my wife has assets that I don't which make her more equipped to care for a baby than me, and I make more so I don't get to stay home with the little ones. When they are old enough, she will return to work and we will share everything. Works fine that way."
- "It takes a village, not just one person."
- "No. Raising children and taking care of a home requires the efforts of multiple people. Women shouldn't have to carry the burden of everything as portrayed in the 1950s."
- "Nah. She can do whatever she wants. If she wants a traditional gender role, fine. If she wants to get a tubal ligation and claw her way up the corporate ladder, that's fine too."

Our last male respondent certainly knows how to create an image with the choice of his words. However, he seems to infer that a woman has only two choices, either assume total responsibility for the childcare and housework, or not have kids and have a successful career. Somehow this respondent doesn't allow for the possibility that a woman could have a family and a career, as is the case with many men.

A look at the results from our female respondents indicate that once again the women don't paint as rosy a picture as the male respondents about men's thoughts on a woman's responsibility for home and childcare.

WOMEN'S RESPONSES

WOMEN RESPONSIBLE CHILDCARE/HOUSEKEEPING	PERCENTAGE
Yes	60
No	24
It Depends	10
I don't know	6

Evidently, our female and male respondents are on opposite ends of the spectrum with their thoughts on a woman's primary responsibility for child and home care. Interestingly, the female respondents mention "babysitting" numerous times, when referencing men's participation in childcare. Here's a few of their comments.

- "Yes, I think that most men believe this. They say they are "looking after" their kids. No-you're the father, act like it."
- "I think that a lot of men have that mindset from how they were raised. Today though a lot of men have gotten out of the women are for cooking, cleaning, and having babies' mentality that they were raised with."
- "I think that most men treat women like slaves and are far more selfish than they will ever admit to themselves."
- "Many if not most have that belief. It becomes obvious when a man says he has to stay home to babysit his children…"
- "Yes, men never call it taking care of my child, they call it babysitting. One doesn't babysit their own children."
- "Not most men today."
- "Not as strongly as a generation ago, but the patterns continue. When a child get sick at school, it's always the mom who is called first, whether she works or not."

There is some resentment indicated in the female respondents' comments. Although it might be comforting to believe that perhaps our female respondents have based their comments on the behavior of men of past generations, that would be a false assumption. Our male and female survey respondents represent ages from the mid-twenties to early eighties. There is even a lone eighteen-year-old respondent. This broad age range ensures a cross-generational sampling.

Perhaps our next and final question, as to whether men's behavior toward women has been influenced by the MeToo movement, will shed some light on whether today's men behave differently toward women compared to the way their fathers acted, and if so, what has caused this shift in sensibilities?

CHAPTER 12

FROM CAVEMEN TO WOKENESS

I'm sure that any baby boomers reading this book remember office flirtations in the workplace during the 1970s, 1980s and 1990s. It was common then to see men and women hugging each other and many women even excelled at telling dirty jokes to their male and female coworkers. Women gave big smiles to men who complimented their appearance. Many of today's marriages are the result of office romances. However, there was a flip side to this freewheeling atmosphere. Some women felt uncomfortable with these interactions but kept these feelings to themselves as they didn't want to look aloof or unfriendly. Although it's likely that most of the men's intentions were innocent, research indicates that as far back as biblical times women were sometimes subjected to unwanted attention from men who had sexual motivations.

Many women suffered silently until in 2006 activist American Tarana Burke first used the phrase *me too* (which became MeToo) on the social media platform Myspace to give a voice to the survivors of sexual violence, harassment, and abuse. Then, in late 2017, the hashtag #MeToo was coined and soon went viral. But before we look at how this movement has influenced men's behavior toward women, we need to listen to the words of our three friends, Jim, Buddy, and Noah to gauge their reactions to the movement.

Jim always speaks respectfully of his mother. He doesn't think that he would be capable of making the many personal sacrifices that she had for the good of her family. Although she was a stay-at-home mom, she instilled in him a deep regard for a woman's autonomy. Jim tells his friends, "I would never sexually force myself on a woman or intimidate her with suggestive comments. I didn't need a movement to teach me that this kind of behavior would be wrong, my upbringing already taught me that lesson. It's not difficult for me to remember this lesson when I interact with women in the workplace. However, I think that in social situations the movement has made me more vigilant about behaviors that I don't really consider sexually charged. As a result, my social contact with women is a little strained. If this keeps sexual predators at bay, then I'm happy to be a little less friendly with women outside of my family members."

Buddy is seething. He turns to Jim and says, "What the hell, Jim! Are you saying that I wasn't raised right? I can't help it if I look at a woman who wears a top-down to her navel and four-inch heels. I wouldn't be a man if I didn't notice her. That MeToo movement just makes a woman think that if a man dumps her then she's safe accusing a guy of something that he didn't do to get back at him. Remember that saying, 'Hell hath no fury like a woman scorned'? We all know that a woman can't appear too eager to get romantic with a guy, or she'll look like a whore. So how am I to know if she really means *no* when I make my move on her or if she's just playing a little hard to get? If women are so pure and looking for a gentle soulmate, then why do they search online dating sites for the hottest-looking guy and bait the men using these sites by posting their most provocative looking photos? The only way that the MeToo movement has affected my behavior with women is that now I don't trust any of them and maybe even hate them a little bit."

Noah sighs at Buddy's tirade. Working in an academic environment has led him to accept all of the principles promoted by the MeToo movement. He carefully chooses his words. "I'm constantly surrounded by young students who believe that activism is a person's obligation. Daily conversations among the students focus on human rights, and the outcry against sexual harassment is loud on college campuses. In my college years, there always was news of fraternities being thrown off campus for sexually abusing women. Now, the younger generation of men are on board with the MeToo movement and can be seen standing in protest shoulder to shoulder with women. I have to admit that when I was a young guy I wouldn't hesitate to give a kiss on the cheek to a female friend, and I thought I was being nice when I told her that she looked great. Now, thanks to my education by a younger generation, I keep my hands to myself and reserve my compliments for my girlfriend, Jane."

Jim says that he wasn't really affected by this movement at all because his mother provided the type of nurturing environment that looked with disdain upon any male behavior that would adversely affect women. Buddy, on the other hand, grew up in an atmosphere where a man was a man, and a woman knew her place. He was affected by the MeToo movement because he feared that a woman would object to his advances or comments. That had to put a damper on his behavior with women. On the other hand, Noah takes pride in wholeheartedly supporting the movement and appears to monitor his behavior to align with the movement's philosophy.

The MeToo movement would have been a very useful tool to end this type of sexual abuse in past decades. In that regard, there is no dearth of examples of this abuse against women that date as far back as biblical times.

YESTERDAY

Apparently, in past eras there was little acknowledgment of the sexual abuse of a woman unless it resulted in rape. As a result, most of the narratives of sexually abused women focus on rape.

The Hebrew Bible emphasized the passivity of abused women not having their voices heard. Dinah, a daughter of Jacob, was raped by a Hivite prince. Even though the prince wanted to marry her, her brothers were outraged that someone would do this to a daughter of Jacob. They wanted retribution, but not because their sister was abused, but because it was an insult to Jacob's family. We never get to hear Dinah's emotions about this horrible experience as her brothers are her spokespersons. But Dinah was lucky in one sense; families back then were not always protective of their female members. Many of the biblical tales recount stories of women who were raped by their brothers.

Things didn't get better for women during ancient Roman times. The veracity of the legend of the "Rape of the Sabine Women" has been debated for centuries and was written by Roman Historian Livy. In Roman mythology this story has become a favorite subject of painters and sculptors.

In the mid-eighth century BC, men of Rome supposedly committed a mass abduction of young women from other cities in the region. Although the title of this subject is the "Rape of the Sabine Women," the use of this word may not mean the same thing as it does today; it is derived from the Latin word *raptio,* which means mass abduction. This might lead us to believe that the Sabine abduction was a kidnapping for ransom, and not a sexual assault. However, as the story goes, during the time of Romulus there weren't enough Romans, and Roman men therefore were encouraged to get a woman pregnant in order to propagate. There was definitely some unwanted sex acts taking place as a result of this mass abduction, so perhaps the modern translation of the word rape should be used in this story. Regardless of whether this is a true story or just a legend, it's a bit disconcerting that this story of sexual abuse continues to be celebrated in the art world. I'm not recommending censorship in art, but it's important that we acknowledge the violence of this subject matter.

Compared to the sexual abuses noted in Greek mythology, the Romans' sexual transgressions seem like mere indiscretions. There are numerous narratives about women being sexually abused by men. Some of the names are familiar, such as Cassandra, Philomela, Hera, and Medusa. The Sabine story was just one of many artistic depictions of sexual abuse of women during classical times.

The rape of Cassandra by Ajax is a favorite scene in Greek art. Cassandra is shown being dragged from the altar of Athena by Ajax who then rapes her. This normalization of rape was so idealized in Greece that a common theme in their stories was of a Greek god such as Zeus, Poseidon, Hades, and Dionysus sexually assaulting human beings and other gods. After Poseidon rapes Demeter, she is advised to lay aside her wrath and go on with her life. Another famous painting portrays the rape of the human Europa by Zeus. Not only weren't these scenarios considered appalling, but they were admired. The MeToo movement would have been very busy in ancient Greek times.

THERE WERE SOME strange punishments meted out for sexual abuse in ancient times, but often the rape victim also was punished. For example, the ancient Assyrians permitted the father of a rape victim to retaliate by raping the wife of the rapist. This was clearly an eye-for-an-eye male retribution with little regard for the female rape victims. The Hebrews were at least headed in the right direction as they punished the rapist. However, they stoned both the rapist and his victim, as it was probably a given that the victim was complicit in her rape. The ancient Greeks viewed rape as a physically violent act against another person with punishments ranging from levying massive fines on the rapist to putting him to death. Nonetheless, as progressive as the ancient Greeks might sound in their thoughts on rape, consent was not a necessity between husband and wife. The writings of Xenophon in the fourth century BC show that the husband controlled his wife's consent regarding sexual relations. An example of the extent of this power is that an older man could choose a younger man to have sex with his wife to produce 'worthy children.'

It wasn't until the sixth century that the Roman Emperor Justinian declared that rape was not simply a defilement of a man's property, but that it was a sexual crime against women. This law applied only to unmarried women as long as they weren't prostitutes. Justinian was aptly named as he was truly a man of justice, that is of course unless you were a married woman who was sexually abused by her husband or farmed out to produce better children.

The ancient civilizations didn't have a stranglehold on the freedom to sexually abuse women, as evidenced in the 1490s with the antics of Christopher Columbus and his men. One of his own men, Michele de Cuneo, proudly recounts how he raped and tortured an indigenous woman. He states that he was given a "Carib woman." He then describes what he did when she fought back against his attempted sexual attacks. He said, "he took a piece of rope and whipped her soundly…finally, we came to an agreement in such a manner that I can tell you she seemed to have been brought up in a school for harlots." I guess that Mr. de Cuneo was invoking the old belief that although at first she protested against his sexual advances, in the end, she showed him that she really liked it.

REMEMBER ALL THOSE movies about slaves during the Civil War? It must have been easy for the producers to get material for those movies because many of the atrocities depicted happened in real-life. Women in slave colonies were routinely raped by their owners. This abuse was not considered assault. Harriot Jacobs was a slave who wrote about her rape in her book, *Incidents in the Life of a Slave Girl, Written by Herself*. She gave birth to two children as a result of being raped, and instead of any punishment her rapist, Samuel Treadwell Sawyer, was elected to Congress.

Recy Taylor wasn't a slave, but that didn't stop six men from gang-raping her when she was walking home from church. This wasn't in ancient times. It was 1944, and yet even though one of the attackers confessed, two white juries refused to indict the accused. This was the South of Jim Crow, and because of the injustice perpetuated on her, the NAACP sent Rosa Parks to investigate. As a result, the Alabama state legislature issued an official apology to Ms. Taylor.

TODAY

Even before the high-profile scandals involving powerful men surfaced during this century, there were some attempts in the twentieth century to seek legal justice for sexual abuse. Unfortunately, after winning in court, a victim's monetary compensation in a sexual abuse verdict was ridiculously low.

It's generally agreed that the first landmark sexual harassment case in America was Barnes v. Train, filed in 1974 in the United States District Court for the District of Columbia. The plaintiff, a Black female, brought the case against her employer, the Environmental Protection Agency, after she lost her job for refusing the sexual advances of a male supervisor. The plaintiff, acting without counsel, mistakenly based her claim on race rather than gender discrimination. At the time, the term *sexual harassment* wasn't used, so the plaintiff didn't know the correct category under which to file her claim. Filing the lawsuit based on race was a mistake, and the case was dismissed. She subsequently secured counsel and filed a new complaint based on sex discrimination. This case was also dismissed. However, in 1977, she appealed the judgment of dismissal and won the appeal and was granted eighteen thousand dollars for lost pay and promotions. The court also ruled that a company is liable if they are aware of sexual harassment by a supervisor. Due to inflation, that settlement would translate to about ninety thousand dollars now. However, in today's MeToo climate, this judgment would be considered a mild slap on the wrist.

The MeToo movement unearthed sexual abuse going back decades. Women were no longer afraid to speak out about the predators who victimized them. The media focused on famous men who were exposed by their victims as they knew that there would be more attention given to these high-profile cases. Because of this heightened awareness, the average woman's cries for justice became more credible. Women realized that if powerful men were being taken down, then their everyday regular guy abusers could also be held responsible for the atrocities they had committed. The stories of these men and their victims could be the subject matter for a separate book, but I'll only highlight a few of the more publicized instances of men using their power and notoriety to abuse women.

Harvey Weinstein, a renowned Hollywood producer, would have felt comfortable living in what was called the golden days of Hollywood where the casting couch was a constant presence in the life of women who wanted to achieve stardom. Back in the day, Harry Cohn, the head of Columbia pictures, also made it clear to aspiring actresses that he expected sex for stardom. Harvey found out soon enough that today's actresses wouldn't comply with his sexual desires. In 2020, he was convicted of rape in the first degree and sentenced to twenty-three years in prison. Clearly, the MeToo movement influenced this retribution.

Bill Cosby was known as America's Dad and one of the funniest comedians in America. Unfortunately, behind the scenes of his hit TV show, Cosby made some sixty women cry by allegedly drugging and sexually abusing them. Supposedly, this abuse was going on for over thirty years, and yet, it wasn't until 2017 that his crimes resulted in a criminal trial. In 2018, Cosby was convicted and sentenced to three - ten years in prison. This verdict was overturned in 2021. Cosby was released after serving nearly three years of his sentence, because, believe it or not, the court said Cosby had made a deal with a prosecutor, resulting in a violation of his due process. Many of you reading this might clamor for that prosecutor's head, but in the end, this unjust decision may not save Cosby. Let's keep our fingers crossed that the several civil lawsuits still pending against Cosby results in justice being served. Many times, in sexual abuse cases it becomes a matter of "he said, she said." However, it's a little difficult to use that reasoning considering that more than sixty women have all essentially alleged the same abuse.

Hollywood is not the only stalking ground of sexual predators as exemplified in the 2018 USA gymnastics sex abuse scandal in which Larry Nassar used his position as team doctor to sexually abuse more than two hundred and sixty young women. He was also convicted and sentenced in three separate jurisdictions for a total of up to one hundred seventy-five years in prison. Although his victims will never be able to wipe out the memories of his abuse, they will be able to take some solace in his punishment.

—

NOT ALL ALLEGATIONS of sexual abuse result in a negative consequence for the alleged perpetrator, as there have been numerous cases of women falsely claiming they've been raped or abused. Such false accusations have been used to try and discredit the MeToo movement, which has been portrayed as anti-male and conducting witch hunts.

Some people also believe that an accused man's life is adversely affected regardless of whether an accusation of sex abuse is true or not. There are several examples of alleged abuse that have either led to no legal consequences or have been quickly dismissed by the courts. The outcome of the events I've noted below should give you some additional food for thought.

The famous chef Mario Batali was accused of groping and forcibly kissing a woman at a Boston restaurant in 2017. He was acquitted in court of the criminal charge because the plaintiff wasn't credible in her testimony. In 2021 Batali, his business partner, and their NYC restaurant agreed to pay six hundred thousand to settle an investigation by the New York attorney general's office over allegations of sexual harassment of employees at his restaurant. One has to wonder why this payment was made if Batali didn't commit harassment.

In 2018, an anonymous accusation was made on the website Babe by a woman who dated the star of the *Master of None* show, Aziz Ansari. The woman claimed that while on a date with him, Ansari pressured her to have sexual intercourse and oral sex. Ansari wrote in a statement to CNN that the sex was consensual and said, "The next day, I got a text from her that said that although it may have seemed okay, upon further reflection, she felt uncomfortable." The woman's statement seems to imply that at the time of the incident she was okay with the sex. If this was the case, then how would Ansari be expected to know she objected to having sexual relations with him if she didn't even know? Charges were never filed.

Some critics of the MeToo movement have charged that the movement is a weaponizing tool used in political attacks. Perhaps the most representative case in point is the sexual allegations against Andrew Cuomo, the ex-governor of the state of New York. In February 2021, the New York State attorney general opened an investigation into the allegations that Cuomo had sexually harassed multiple women during his time in office. He denied the accusations and resigned. Cuomo insisted that because of his Italian heritage, he considered hugging and kissing people a natural, non-sexual thing. Cuomo was often a lone ranger in his political party. He made a practice of following his own counsel, which sometimes meant that he would oppose the party line. He claimed that the Democrat Party was using these false sexual accusations as a political vendetta. Cuomo grew up during a time when social conventions regarding interactions between men and women were quite different. Did these generational differences and his Italian heritage lead to his political demise, or was he really a ruthless sexual predator? There is no way to answer this question, as Cuomo was never prosecuted.

I'm sure that by now you are either sputtering with outrage over some of these stories because you think that a bad guy got away with something, or you think that the unfortunate thing about these narratives is that some innocent men are getting trapped in the net of the MeToo fervor. The last question in our survey will provide us with our male respondents' answers to the question of whether their behavior has been affected by the MeToo movement.

MEN'S RESPONSES

HAS METOO CHANGED MEN'S BEHAVIOR	PERCENTAGE
Yes	26
No	67
I don't know	7

The responses overwhelmingly indicate that most of our male respondents felt no influence on their behavior from the MeToo movement. Either these men were always candidates for sainthood and didn't need the movement to act in the correct way with women, or they believe that no one, including the courts, has the right to tell them what to do. Let's look at some of the reasons that they gave for their opinions.

- "Not really. I don't agree with every aspect of MeToo. I think it puts too much emphasis on women always telling the truth, when no group of humans always tells the truth. I think we have seen examples where accusations were shown to be incorrect, and too much knee jerk reacting was done."
- "It caused me to trust women less."
- "Yes, more careful to ensure I am not alone with a woman who isn't my wife or family and no physical contact: hugs, etc."
- "Nope. Never felt the need to do creepy things."
- "Slightly. I used to have a rule that I would never touch a woman at work (e.g., tap on the arm). But I've become even more restrictive since MeToo. For example, I deliberately avoid using certain words with women or sharing certain research findings with them because they could misunderstand my intentions. I also never go to one-on-one lunches with women anymore."
- "Yes. I do not believe all acts are 'sexual harassment' and we

cannot keep redrawing the line. My concern with the movement is where it is used as a sword rather than a shield."
- "No, my behavior is based on how I was raised."
- "Nope, I've always treated women right, that's how I was raised."
- "No, I'm not a pig."
- "Makes me more understanding of what I was too blind to see."
- "I am less likely to approach a woman to talk. I feel like all women think all men are rapists now. I'll probably start dating guys now because women just don't want sex anymore."

The last respondent's comment is an attempt at humor, but nonetheless his remark shows that the MeToo movement has definitely influenced his behavior toward women. The remaining comments indicate that the majority of men who answered no to the question attribute their answer to the fact that their upbringing taught them not to sexually abuse women. Now let's see if our female respondents agree with our men on the question of how the MeToo movement influenced the men's lives.

WOMEN'S RESPONSES

HAS METOO CHANGED MEN'S BEHAVIOR	PERCENTAGE
Yes	48
No	26
It Depends	2
I don't know	24

The female respondents' answers are vastly divergent from those of the male respondents. The females believe that the men were tremendously influenced by the MeToo movement, although not always in a positive way. The words fear, hostility, and aggression constantly come up in the female respondents' comments to indicate how men were affected. The comments below reference these emotions numerous times.

- "Yes, I think that men who don't fully understand what constitutes sexual harassment are now afraid to interact with women at all for fear of offending them. They would rather not take a chance that they could be misunderstood, instead of understanding the root of the problem and changing their own behavior."
- "Yes, makes some of them more dangerous."
- "I think it brought awareness and made some men want to step up. While others felt threatened and try to counter the movement."
- "I'm not sure, however I suspect there have been behavior changes put into place to protect themselves, not out of concern for women."
- "I think it made them more skeptical, not better behaved."
- "For the ones that were predators. Not at all. They may have become more discrete."
- "I think it influenced their behavior but probably not their attitudes. I think that males would continue to objectify women if they thought they could get away with it."

As you can see, the female respondents have qualified their yes answers with many somewhat unflattering motivations underlying the reasons for the influence of the MeToo movement on men.

The topic of the MeToo movement's influence has the potential to change a civil conversation among friends into heated fights. Maybe turning to objective research will help to resolve some of these disagreements.

The Pew Research Center has published a study containing the results of a survey of about six thousand adults in the United States to find out how the MeToo movement has affected men and women in the workplace. Sixty-six percent of those participating in the survey said it increased focus on sexual abuse in the workplace and has made men anxious about interacting with women. Only 20 percent stated they felt more comfortable working with women. Generational differences were noted as adults ages eighteen to twenty-nine were 64 percent most likely to support the movement. Evidently, as our survey shows, the MeToo movement has affected men, although not always in a way that makes all men happy.

Men from different generations, cultures, races, professions, ages, economic backgrounds, and educational levels have told us what they really think about women. However, the question of why they think the way they do still needs to be answered. Maybe we'll find those answers in our Afterword.

AFTERWORD

WE HAVEN'T TOTALLY shattered the wall of silence that has prevented men from voicing their true sentiments about women. We have, however, through our travels dating from biblical to modern times, removed a big enough chunk of this wall to be able to get a small peek into WHAT men REALLY think about women. Now, we are left with only one question: Why do men think the way they do?

According to historical narratives and our survey results, there appears to be a few main factors that shape the way men think about women. These factors are upbringing, life experiences, societal customs, and education.

There always will be arguments of nature vs. nurture in a discussion of the determinant of a person's behavior. An example of this is a student who has attained high levels of academic success. Is this student's intelligence due to a genetic predisposition, or does it stem from growing up in an intellectually stimulating environment? Many men in our survey attribute their upbringing as the basis for their opinions on women. In families in which the power structure's hierarchy designates the male as supreme power and delegates women to subordinate roles, men are more likely to think that they are biologically predetermined to aggressively use a woman as a tool to obtain their goals.

On the other hand, a man is less likely to engage in misogynistic behavior if his upbringing models for him a dynamic that demonstrates respect and balance in male-female relationships.

Life experiences can have a tremendous impact on a man raised in even the most nurturing home. Imagine this scenario. A man is waiting in a small room to be called into a church where over one hundred people are gathered to witness his marriage to the girl of his dreams. Suddenly, he notices a text on his phone from his fiancée. She has sent him a short note which says, "I've changed my mind. I can't marry you because I've been having an affair with your best man and plan on marrying him." Obviously, the callowness of his fiancée's message will probably have a major effect on this man's ability to trust women in the future.

Another example is that of a man who recently started a new job. His boss is a woman. In the short time that he's been employed at his new company, he has been relieved to see that she treats all her employees equally. Everyone in the office extols her accomplishments and tells stories of her superlative administrative skills. This woman tries to dispel any negative associations that her employees might have previously held about working under a woman. Our new male employee in this narrative will probably have a vastly different impression of women than the impression of our jilted groom to be.

Prior to 1995, men and women would meet and talk for a bit before deciding whether they wanted to date. The first online dating website changed all of that. The swipe of a finger can now determine the potential for a possible romantic relationship. This experience has led many men to believe that women are only interested in a man if he has Hollywood looks and tons of money.

—

THROUGHOUT HISTORY, SOCIALLY constructed gender roles have played a major part in maintaining the double standard of acceptable behavior between the sexes. Society has labeled strong women unfeminine and aggressive, while powerful men receive pats on the back and promotions in the workplace. Because of gender bias in society, the ideal woman has historically been described as submissive, chaste, and subordinate to a man. This false depiction results in the belief of some men that women are created for their benefit and that women are all breathlessly waiting to be ravished by a man. Unfortunately, this type of thinking leads to many incidents of sexual abuse.

The power of education can be beautifully described in the quote from Nelson Mandela that states, "Education is the most powerful weapon which you can use to change the world." Following this line of thought, it's easy to see that education would have a tremendous impact on a man's perspective about women. A Pew study of around forty-five hundred adults was conducted in 2017. This study revealed that one-third of men without a college degree saw themselves as very masculine, while less than one-fourth of male college graduates identified themselves at the same level of masculinity. It's likely that the men who felt more masculine might be conforming to traditional societal mandates of masculine roles, which emphasize strength and emotional restraint for men.

Progressive ideas explored during college years could result in a male student's rejection of long-established ideologies and, subsequently, affect his attitude toward women. Several studies have shown that men who adhere to traditional masculine gender norms are more likely to perpetrate acts of sexual abuse toward their partners. Strangely enough, these same studies also indicate that men who fail to live up to society's vision of masculinity also commit acts of abuse in their relationships with women to compensate for feelings of impotence and inadequacy. In the end, it's difficult to ascertain if a man's education adversely or advantageously affects his thoughts about women.

The Chinese philosophical concept of yin and yang might best describe the dichotomy between men and women. It describes the existence of opposite but interconnected forces. Men and women are living examples of this principle. We can all agree that men and women are very different from one another, and yet it's undeniable that they are interconnected. Perhaps many of the clashes between the sexes would vanish if both genders acknowledged their unique qualities and worked toward fitting them together to achieve their joint goals.

Finally, to all the men and women who have read this book, I want to leave you with a call to action. I want you to promise that if you encounter walls of silence don't be afraid to stand up and do your best to knock those walls down. Then women will no longer have to wonder, "What does he really think about me." Instead, they'll have a decision to make. Will they try to fulfill the expectations of the men in their lives, or will they need to find new men?

DEMOGRAPHICS
FEMALE RESPONDENTS

OCCUPATION	RACE	EDUCATION
35% Management	93% Caucasian	49% College
26% Non-Management	4% African American/Black	28% Post Graduate
17% Other	3% Asian	21% High School
12% Professional		2% Non-Responsive
6% Unemployed		
3% Retired		
1% IT		
INCOME	RELIGION	COUNTRY/REGION
21% Under $50,000	22% Catholic	26% South USA
19% $ $50,000-$100,000	20% Christian	25% Midwest USA
48% Over $100,000	19% Jewish	21% North East USA
2% Over $200,000	18% Protestant	17% West USA
10% No response	13% Atheist	8% USA
	4% Agnostic	3% International
	4% No response	

DEMOGRAPHICS
MALE RESPONDENTS

OCCUPATION	RACE	EDUCATION
12% Management	46% Caucasian	50% College
27% Non-Management	19% African American/Black	27% Post Graduate
14% Other	16% Asian	17% High School
17% Professional	11% Latino	6% Non-Responsive
2% Unemployed	8% Other	
23% Retired		
5% IT		

INCOME	RELIGION	COUNTRY/REGION
32% Under $50,000	29% Jewish	37% North East USA
32% $50,000-$100,000	27% Catholic	16% International
22% $100,000-$200,000	13% Protestant	13% South USA
2% Over $200,000	13% Agnostic	12% West USA
12% No response	9% Atheist	11% Midwest USA
	5% Other	7% USA
	4% No response	4% Other

Acknowledgments

THE BIGGEST THANKS goes to my husband who I'm sure took a deep breath when I announced that I would be writing my second book. I know that he was happy when the first book was published, as it must have gotten frustrating when I had very little time for normal family responsibilities. Now, here we were doing it all over again. My husband was invaluable in stopping me from throwing in commas into every phrase and reminding me to check my flow of thoughts. Although there were moments when I know he wanted me and my book to disappear, he was always there for me. Thank you, John, for all the help you gave me. As before, I never could have done this without you.

I appreciate my children for patiently listening to me whenever I excitedly reiterated to them something about a topic I'd researched that I'm sure bored them to death. I'm especially grateful to my sons Chris, Jason, and Don, who didn't hang up the phone on me when I called them with numerous cries for help over a formatting question, and to my daughter, Jennifer, who was a shoulder to lean on when I became exasperated with the process.

Although they're not around to read this book, I know that my parents would be proud of my tenacity in not giving up my dreams of being a writer. I thank them for making me believe I could do anything.

Bibliography

Alsop, Gulielma Fell. 1950. *History of the Woman's Medical College, Philadelphia, Pennsylvania, 1850–1950.* Philadelphia: Lippincott

Blow, Adrian, Tina M. Timm & Ronald Cox (2008) *The Role of the Therapist in Therapeutic Change: Does Therapist Gender Matter?,* Journal of Feminist Family Therapy, 20:1, 66-86, DOI: 10.1080/08952800801907150

Brown, Anna. 09/29/2022. *More Than Twice as Many Americans Support Than Oppose the #MeToo Movement.* Washington, D.C. Pew Research Center

Cerrato, J. & Cifre, E. 2018. *Gender Inequality in Household Chores and Work-Family Conflict.* Frontiers in Psychology,9. https://doi.org/10.3389/fpsyg.2018.01330

Cottone, J. G., Drucker, P., & Javier, R. A. (2002). *Gender differences in psychotherapy dyads: Changes in psychological symptoms and responsiveness to treatment during 3 months of therapy. Psychotherapy: Theory, Research, Practice, and Training, 39,* 297-308. American Psychological Association. https://psycnet.apa.org

Deseret News. *Mothers of Famous People/Lincoln.*05/12/2006. https://www.deseret.com

Grant, Mary. Hyginus, 2019. *Gaius Julius, Fabulae* translation. https://topostext.org

Godefrey, Neale. July 31, 2017. Forbes. https://www. Forbes.com

Griffis, William Elliott. *The Mikado's empire: A History of Japan from the age of Gods to the Meiji Era (660BC-AD1872)* April 1, 2007. Stone Bridge Press.

Hass, Maya, November 4, 2020. *Prehistoric Female Hunter Discovery Upends Gender Role Assumptions. National Geographic*

Hewlett, Sylvia Ann. April 2022. *Executive Women and the Myth of Having It All. Harvard Business Review.*

Ipsos Flair Japan Collection. *The Devil You Know.* 2022 https://www.ipsos.com

King, Gilbert. *History/the Latin lover and his enemies.* July 13, 2012. https://.www.smithsonianmag.com

Lecoq, Titiou. *Feminism & French Women in History: A Resource Guide.* 2015. The Library of Congress, https://guides.loc.gov

Lopes Maria and Julia Inuma, Older Japanese Men Lost In the Kitchen, Turn To Housework School, November 25, 2022, Washington Post

Masci, David. *The Divide Over Ordaining Women.* September 9, 2014. Pew Research Center

National at Home Dad Network. https://www.athomedad.org

Parker, Kim & Juliana Menasce Horowitz, and Renee Stepler. *On Gender differences no consensus on Nature vs Nurture.* December 5, 2017. Pew Research Center.

Reidy, Dennis E., Danielle S. Berke, Brittany Gentile and Amos Eichner. *Man Enough? Masculine discrepancy stress and intimate partner violence by men.* March 26,2018. PubMed Central. https://www.ncbi.nlm.nih.gov

Respers, Lisa. Aziz Ansari talks about sexual misconduct in his new Netflix special and people have feelings. July 10, 2019. France. https://www.cnn.com

Retief. F.P. 2006.Supplementum 7. *The Healing Hand: the Role of Women in Ancient Medicine-*African Journals online. https:www.ajol.info.

Science. May 15, 2015. Vol 348.Issue 6236. Pp. 796-798

Schutte, Shan. *Facebook CEO Mark Zuckerberg's Advice For Women, Don't Date The Nerd Be the Nerd.* January 7, 2016. https://www.realbusiness.com.uk

Sherman, Ted. N.J Advance Media. *Elite, secretive N.J. golf club unlawfully banned women from playing, owning houses, complaint says.* February 16, 2023. https://www.mj.com

Smith, Simone Haruko. *Dante's Divine Purpose-Reflections on Dante Alighieri's "Paradiso.,"* July 18, 2022. https://www.owlcation.com

Spencer. Erika Hope. *Feminism & French Women in History: A Resource Guide.* August 1, *2021.*The Library of Congress, https://guides.loc.gov

Surpless, Emily. *Things You Didn't Know About Oprah's Boyfriend.* August 15,2019. https://www.nickiswift.com

Walsh, Mary Roth. *Doctors Wanted: No Women Need Apply: Sexual Barriers in the Medical Profession, 1835–1975* CT:1977. Yale University Press.

Warner, C.D. et al. *Letter to the King of Prussia.1917.* https://www.bartleby.com

Winston, Aaron R. *A timeline of the Bill Cosby Case Accuser Lawsuit.* September 2, 2022, https://www.expresslegalfunding.com

Wintersteen, M. B., Mensinger, J. L., & Diamond, G. S. (2005*). Do gender and racial differences between patient and therapist affect therapeutic alliance and treatment retention in adolescents? Psychology Research and Practice, 6,* 400-408.

Zaggo care. *Should you use a female doctor? Does gender matter?* December 5, 2021. https://www.zaggocare.org

Zippia. *Primary Care Physician Demographics and Statistics in the U.S.2021.* https://www.zippia.com

www.ingramcontent.com/pod-product-compliance
Lightning Source LLC
LaVergne TN
LVHW091542070526
838199LV00002B/170